DANSE MACABRE:

The
Dance of Death

Art by Hans Holbein the Younger

Engraved by Hans Lützelburger
Quatrains by Gilles Corrozet or Jean de Vauzelles
Introduction by Austin Dobson
Translation by Lawrence Knorr

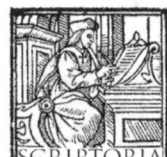

an imprint of Sunbury Press, Inc.
Mechanicsburg, PA USA

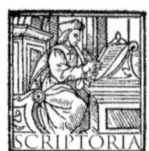

an imprint of Sunbury Press, Inc.
Mechanicsburg, PA USA

For information about special discounts for bulk purchases, please contact Sunbury Press Orders Dept. at (855) 338-8359 or orders@sunburypress.com.

To request one of our authors for speaking engagements or book signings, please contact Sunbury Press Publicity Dept. at publicity@sunburypress.com.

FIRST SCRIPTORIA PRESS EDITION: January 2021

Set in Adobe Garamond | Interior design by Crystal Devine | Cover design by Lawrence Knorr | Edited by Lawrence Knorr.

Publisher's Cataloging-in-Publication Data
Names: Holbein, Hans, artist.
Title: Danse macabre : the dance of death / Hans Holbein the Younger.
Description: First trade paperback edition. | Mechanicsburg, PA : Scriptoria Press, 2021.
Summary: Hans Holbein's timeless artwork reminding us of our mortality, regardless of our station in life, are reproduced at over four times the size of the original prints. This edition is newly edited and includes appropriate Bible verses.
Identifiers: ISBN : 978-1-620065-04-4 (softcover).
Subjects: ART / European | ART / History / Renaissance | ART / Individual Artists / Artists' Books | ART / Subjects & Themes / Religious | RELIGION / Christian Living / Death, Grief, Bereavement.

Product of the United States of America
0 1 1 2 3 5 8 13 21 34 55

Continue the Enlightenment!

THE BOOK

*L*es Simulachres & Historiées Faces de la Mort avtant elegamtment pourtraictes, que artificiellement imaginées. This may be Englished as follows: *The Images and Storied Aspects of Death, as elegantly delineated as [they are] ingeniously imagined.* Such is the literal title of the earliest edition of the famous book, familiarly known as *Holbein's Dance of Death.* It is a small quarto, bearing on its title page, below the French words above quoted, a nondescript emblem with the legend *Vsus me Genuit,* and on an open book, *Gnothe seauton.* Below this comes again, "*A Lyon, Soubz l'escu de Coloigne*: M. D. XXXVIII," while at the end of the volume is the imprint "*Excvdebant Lvgdvni Melchoir et Gaspar Trechsel fratres: 1538,*"—the Trechsels being printers of German origin, who had long been established at Lyons. There is a verbose "Epistre" or Preface in French to the "*moult reuerende Abbesse du religieux conuent S. Pierre de Lyon, Madame Iehanne de Touszele,*" otherwise the Abbess of Saint Pierre les Nonnains, a religious house containing many noble and wealthy ladies, and the words, "*Salut d'un vray Zèle,*" which conclude the dedicatory heading, are supposed to reveal indirectly the author of the "Epistre" itself, namely, Jean de Vauzelles, Pastor of St. Romain and Prior of Monrottier, one of three famous literary brothers in the city on the Rhone, whose motto was "*D'un vray Zelle.*" After the Preface comes "*Diuerses Tables de Mort, non painctes, mais extraictes de l'escripture saincte, colorées par Docteurs Ecclesiastiques, & umbragées par Philosophes.*" Then follow the cuts, forty-one in number, each having its text from the Latin Bible above it, and below, its quatrain in French, this latter is understood to be from the pen of one Gilles Corozet. To the cuts succeed various makeweight Appendices of a didactic and hortatory character, the whole being wound up by a profitable discourse, *De la Necessite de la Mort qui ne laisse riens estre pardurable.* Various editions ensued to this first one of 1538, the next or second of 1542 (in which Corozet's verses were translated into Latin by Luther's brother-in-law, George Oemmel or Aemilius), being put forth by Jean and François Frellon, into whose hands the establishment of the Trechsels had fallen. There were subsequent issues in 1545, 1547, 1549, 1554, and 1562. To the issues of 1545 and 1562 a few supplementary designs were added, some of which have no special bearing upon the general theme, although attempts, more or less ingenious, have been made to connect them with the text. After 1562 no addition was made to the plates.

THE ARTIST

From the date of the *editio princeps* it might be supposed that the designs were executed at or about 1538—the year of its publication. But this is not the case, and there is good evidence that they were not only designed but cut on the wood some eleven years before the book itself was published. There are, in fact, several sets of impressions in the British Museum, the Berlin Museum, the Basle Museum, the Imperial Library at Paris, and the Grand Ducal Cabinet at Carlsruhe, all of which correspond with each other and are believed to be engraver's proofs from the original blocks. These, which include every cut in the edition of 1538, except "The Astrologer," would prove little of themselves as to the date of execution. Luckily, there is in the Cabinet at Berlin a set of coarse enlarged drawings in Indian ink, on brownish paper, of twenty-three of the series. These are in circular form; and were apparently intended as sketches for glass painting. That they are copied from the woodcuts is demonstrable, first, because they are not reversed as they would have been if they were the originals; and, secondly, because one of them, No. 36 ("The Duchess"), repeats the conjoined "H.L." on the bed, which initials are held to be the monogram of the woodcutter, and not to be part of the original design. The Berlin drawings must therefore have been executed subsequently to the woodcuts. As one of them, representing the Emperor, is dated 1527, we get a date before which both the woodcuts and the designs for the woodcuts must have been prepared. It is generally held that they were so prepared circa 1524 and 1525, the date of the Peasants' War, of the state of feeling excited by which they exhibit evident traces. In the Preface to this first edition, certain ambiguous expressions, to which we shall presently refer, led some of the earlier writers on the subject to doubt as to the designer of the series. But the later research of Wornum and Woltmann, of M. Paul Mantz and, more recently, of Mr. W. J. Linton leaves no doubt that they were drawn by the artist to whom they have always been traditionally assigned, to wit, Hans Holbein the younger. He was resident in Basle up to the autumn of 1526, before which time, according to the above argument, the drawings must have been produced; he had already designed an Alphabet of Death; moreover, on the walls of the cemetery of the Dominican monastery at Basle, there was a famous wall-painting of the Dance of Death, which would be a perpetual stimulus to any resident artist. Finally, this is perhaps the most important consideration; the designs are in Holbein's manner.

THE WOODCUTTER

But besides revealing an inventor of the highest order, the *Dance of Death* also discloses an interpreter in wood of signal, and even superlative, ability. The designs are cut—to use the word which implies the employment of the knife as opposed to that of the graver—in a manner which has never yet been excelled. In this matter, there could be no better judge than Mr. W. J. Linton, and he says that nothing, either by knife or by graver, is of higher quality than these woodcuts. Yet the woodcutter's very name was doubtful for a long time, and even now, the particulars we possess concerning him are scanty and inconclusive. That he was dead when the Trechsels published the book in 1538 must be inferred from the "Epistre" of Jean de Vauzelles, since that "Epistre" expressly refers to "*la mort de celluy, qui nous en a icy imaginé si elegantes figures*"; and without entering into elaborate enquiry as to the exact meaning of "*imaginer*" in sixteenth-century French, it is obvious that, although the deceased is elsewhere loosely called "*painctre*," this title cannot refer to Holbein, who was so far from being dead that he survived until 1543. The only indication of the woodcutter's name is supplied by the monogram, "HL" upon the bedstead in No. 36 ("The Duchess"); and these initials have been supposed to indicate one Hans Lutzelburger or Hans of Luxemburg, "otherwise Franck," a form-cutter ("formschneider"), whose full name is to be found attached to the so-called "Little Dance of Death," an alphabet by Holbein, impressions of which are in the British Museum. His signature ("H. L. F. 1522") is also found appended to another alphabet, to a cut of a fight in a forest, dated 1522, and an engraved title page in a German New Testament of the year following. This is all we know with certainty concerning his work. However, Dr. Édouard His's investigations have established the fact that a "formschneider" named Hans, who had business transactions with the Trechsels of Lyons, had died at Basle before June 1526. It is conjectured, though absolute proof is not forthcoming, that this must have been the "H. L.," or Hans of Luxemburg, who cut Holbein's designs upon the wood. In any case, unless we must assume another woodcutter of equal merit, the same man probably cut the signed Alphabet in the British Museum and the initialed *Dance of Death*. But why the cuts of the latter, which, as we have shown above, were printed circa 1526, were not published at Lyons until 1538; and why Holbein's name was withheld in the Preface to the book of that year, are still unexplained. The generally accepted supposition is that motives of timidity, arising from the satirical and fearlessly unsparing character of the designs, may be answerable both for the delay in the publication and mystification in the "Preface." And if intentional mystification is admitted, the doors of enquiry, after three hundred and fifty years, are practically sealed to the critical picklock.

OTHER REPRODUCTIONS

The *Dance of Death* has been frequently copied. Mr. W. J. Linton enumerates a Venice reproduction of 1545; and a set (enlarged) by Jobst Dienecker of Augsburg in 1554. Then there is the free copy, once popular with our great grandfathers, by Bewick's younger brother John, which Hodgson of Newcastle published in 1789 under the title of *Emblems of Mortality*. Wenceslaus Hollar etched thirty of the designs in 1651, and in 1788 forty-six of them were etched by David Deuchar. In 1832 they were reproduced upon stone with great care by Joseph Schlotthauer, Professor in the Academy of Fine Arts at Munich, and these were reissued in this country in 1849 by John Russell Smith. They have also been rendered in photolithography for an edition issued by H. Noel Humphreys in 1868 and for the Holbein Society in 1879. In 1886, Dr. F. Lippmann edited for Mr. Quaritch a set of reproductions of the engraver's proofs in the Berlin Museum; and the *editio princeps* has been facsimiled by one of the modern processes for Hirth of Munich, as vol. x. of the Liebhaber-Bibliothek, 1884.

THE PRESENT ISSUE

The copies given in the present issue are impressions from the blocks engraved in 1833 for Douce's *Holbein's Dance of Death*. They are the best imitations in wood, says Mr. Linton. It is, of course, true, as he also points out, that a copy with the graver can never quite faithfully follow an original which has been cut with the knife—more especially, it may be added when the cutter is a supreme craftsman like him of Luxemburg. But against etched, lithographed, phototyped, and otherwise-processed copies, these of Messrs. Bonner and John Byfield have one incontestable advantage: they are honest attempts to repeat by the same method—that is, in wood—the original and incomparable woodcuts of Hans Lutzelburger.

For this 2021 edition, the image descriptions and quatrains from Corozet are translated into English. Bible verses present in some editions of the work have been added, as have eight additional images.

THE DANCE OF DEATH

(CHANT ROYAL, AFTER HOLBEIN)[1]

"Contra vim Mortis
Non est medicamen in hortis."

He is the despots' Despot. All must bide,
Later or soon, the message of his might;
Princes and potentates their heads must hide,
Touched by the awful sigil of his right;
Beside the Kaiser he at eve doth wait
And pours a potion in his cup of state;
The stately Queen his bidding must obey;
No keen-eyed Cardinal shall him affray;
And to the Dame that wantoneth he saith—
"Let be, Sweet-heart, to junket and to play."
There is no king more terrible than Death.

The lusty Lord, rejoicing in his pride,
He draweth down; before the armèd Knight
With jingling bridle-rein he still doth ride;
He crosseth the strong Captain in the fight;
The Burgher grave he beckons from debate;
He hales the Abbot by his shaven pate,
Nor for the Abbess' wailing will delay;
No bawling Mendicant shall say him nay;
E'en to the pyx the Priest he followeth,
Nor can the Leech his chilling finger stay . . .
There is no king more terrible than Death.

All things must bow to him. And woe betide
The Wine-bibber,—the Roisterer by night;
Him the feast-master, many bouts defied,
Him 'twixt the pledging and the cup shall smite;

Woe to the Lender at usurious rate,
The hard Rich Man, the hireling Advocate;
Woe to the Judge that selleth right for pay;
Woe to the Thief that like a beast of prey
With creeping tread the traveller harryeth:—
These, in their sin, the sudden sword shall slay . . .
There is no king more terrible than Death.

He hath no pity,—nor will be denied.
When the low hearth is garnishèd and bright,
Grimly he flingeth the dim portal wide,
And steals the Infant in the Mother's sight;
He hath no pity for the scorned of fate:—
He spares not Lazarus lying at the gate,
Nay, nor the Blind that stumbleth as he may;
Nay, the tired Ploughman,—at the sinking ray,—
In the last furrow,—feels an icy breath,
And knows a hand hath turned the team astray . . .
There is no king more terrible than Death.

He hath no pity. For the new-made Bride,
Blithe with the promise of her life's delight,
That wanders gladly by her Husband's side,
He with the clatter of his drum doth fright;
He scares the Virgin at the convent grate;

The Maid half-won, the lover passionate;
He hath no grace for weakness and decay:
The tender Wife, the Widow bent and gray,
The feeble Sire whose footstep faltereth,—
All these he leadeth by the lonely way . . .
There is no king more terrible than Death.

---

[1] This Chant Royal of the King of Terrors is—with Mr. Austin Dobson's consent—here reprinted from his Collected Poems, 1896.

Les ſimulachres &

HISTORIEES FACES

DE LA MORT, AVTANT ELE

gammēt pourtraictes, que artifi‐
ciellement imaginées.

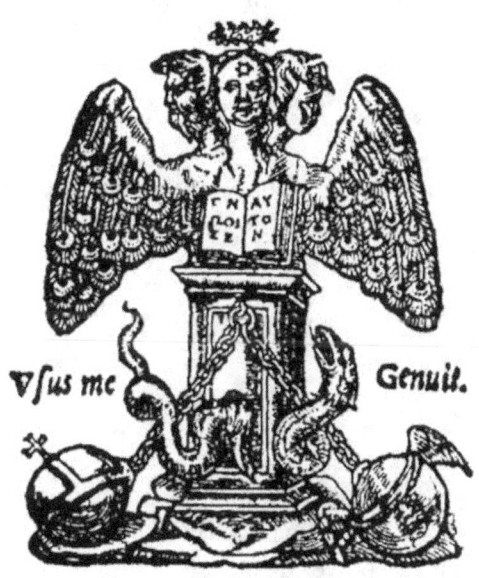

Vſus me   Genuit.

A LYON,

Soubz l'eſcu de COLOIGNE,

M. D. XXXVIII.

I

THE CREATION

Die Schöpfung aller Ding.

Eve is taken from the side of Adam.

And the Lord God formed man of the dust of the ground.

GENESIS 2:7

In the image of God created He him; male and female created He them.

GENESIS 1:7

God made the Heavens, the Sea, the Earth,
O'er Chaos endless power displayed,
And from the dust—the dust of Earth—
Both man and woman in His image made.

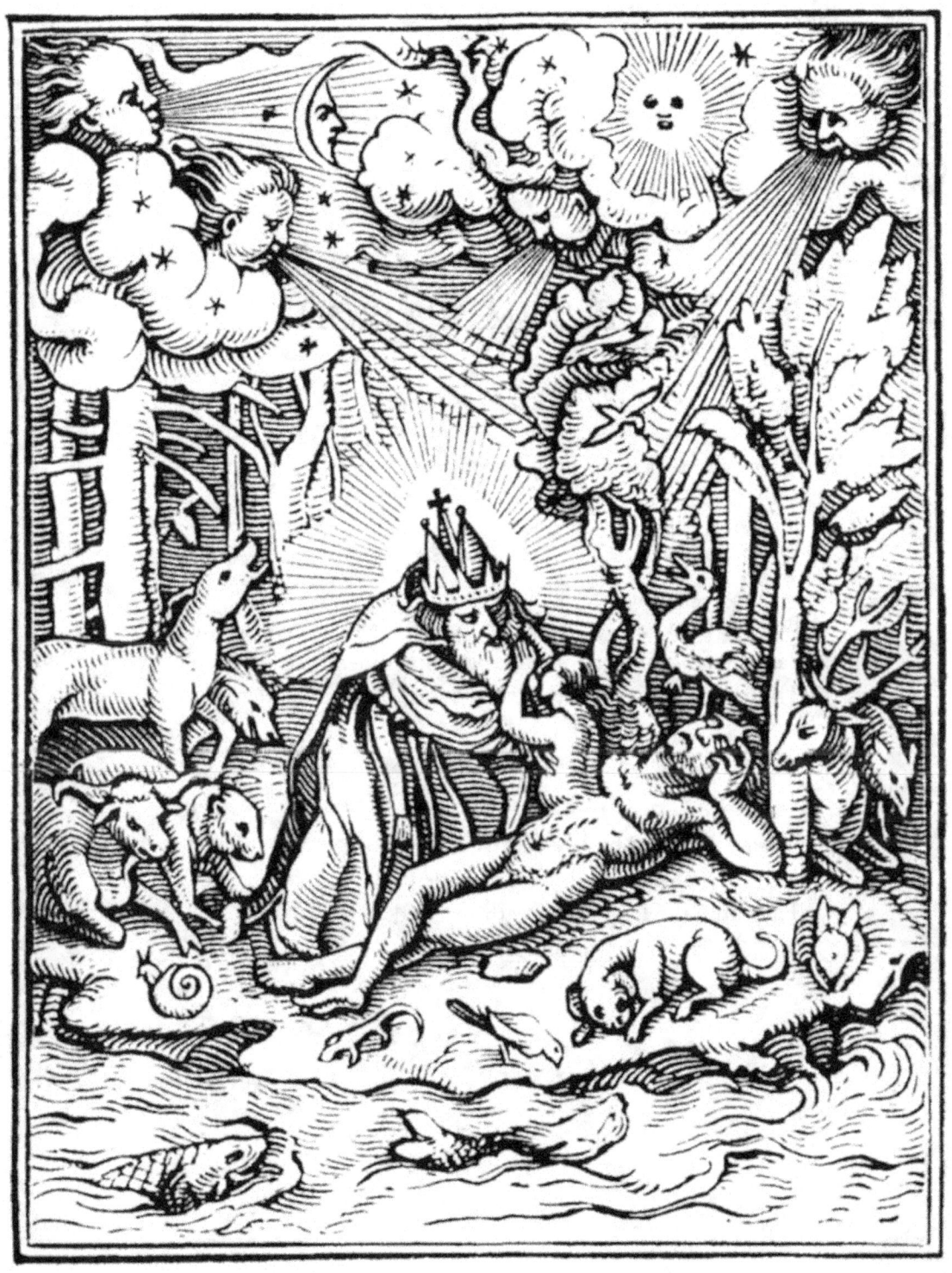

II

THE TEMPTATION

"Adam Eua im Paradyss."

Eve, having received an apple from the serpent, prompts Adam to gather more.

Because thou hast hearkened unto the voice of thy wife, and
hast eaten of the tree, of which I commanded thee, saying,
Thou shalt not wat of it.

GENESIS 3:17

When Adam was by Eve deceived,
And ate the fruit which God forbade,
They both the Doom of Death received,
And all man's race was mortal made.

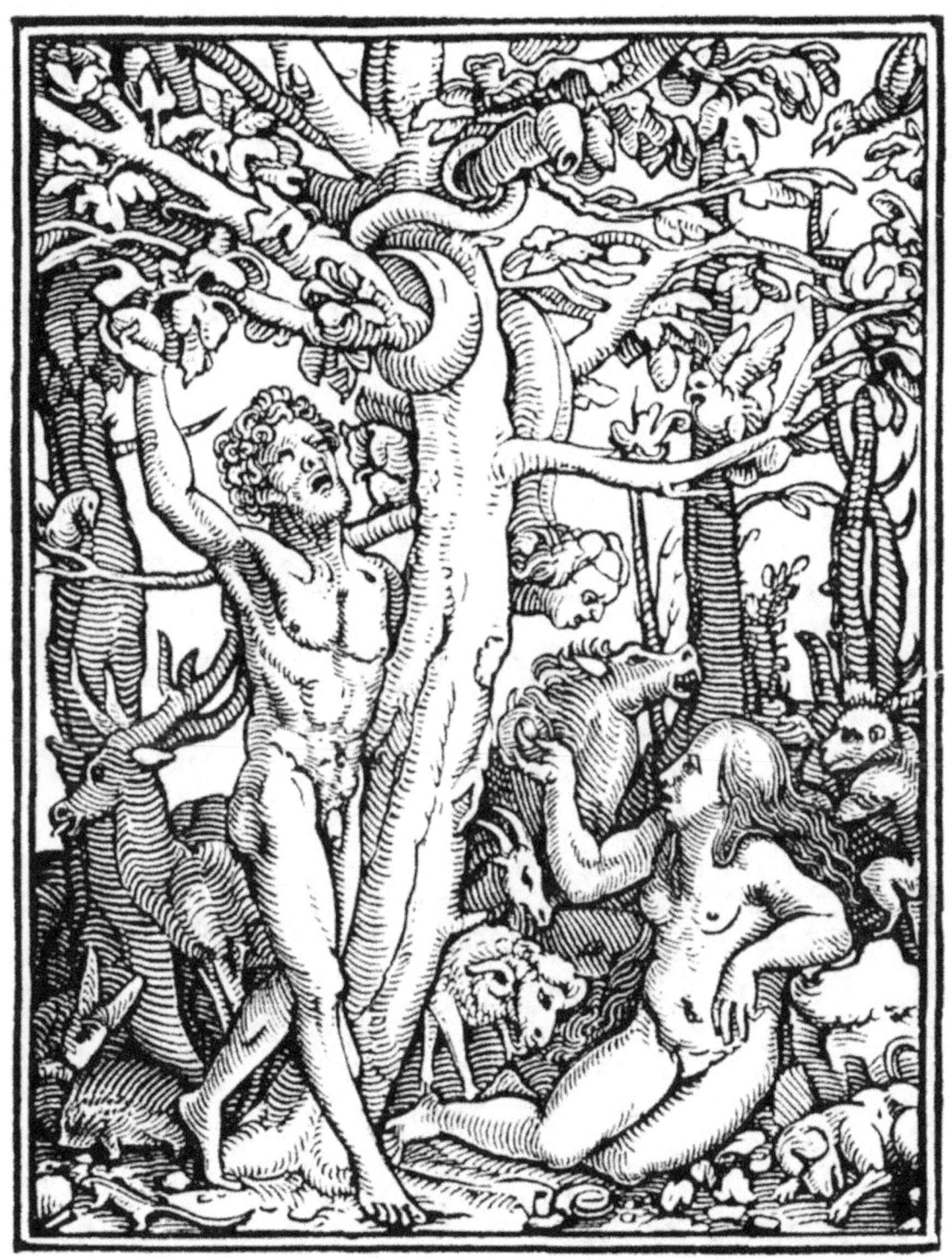

III

THE EXPULSION FROM PARADISE

"Vsstribung Ade Eue."

Adam and Eve, preceded by Death, playing on a beggar's lyre or hurdy-gurdy, are driven by the angel from Eden.

Therefore, the Lord God sent him forth from the garden of
Eden, to the ground from whence he was taken.

GENESIS 3:23

So God drove man from Paradise,
By daily toil to win his bread;
And Death came forth to claim his prize,
And number all men with the dead.

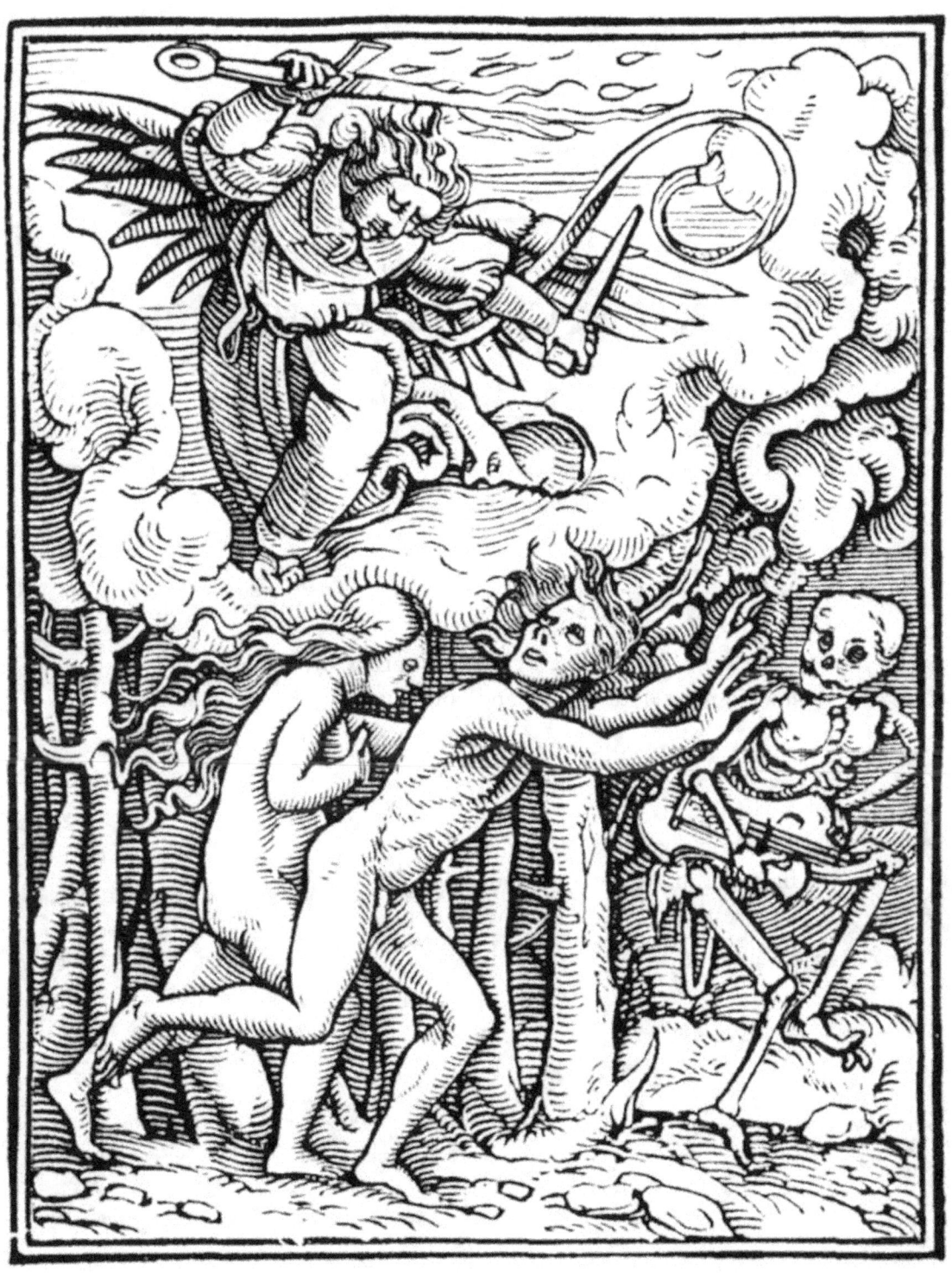

IV

THE CONSEQUENCES OF THE FALL

Adam baut die Erden.

Adam, aided by Death, tills the earth. Eve, with a distaff, suckles Cain in the background.

Cursed is the ground for thy sake; in sorrow shalt thou eat of
it all the days of thy life … and unto dust shalt thou return.

GENESIS 3:17 & 19

Cursed in they toil shall earth be found,
In labour shall thy days be pass'd;
Till Death shall thrust the underground,
Returning dust to dust at last.

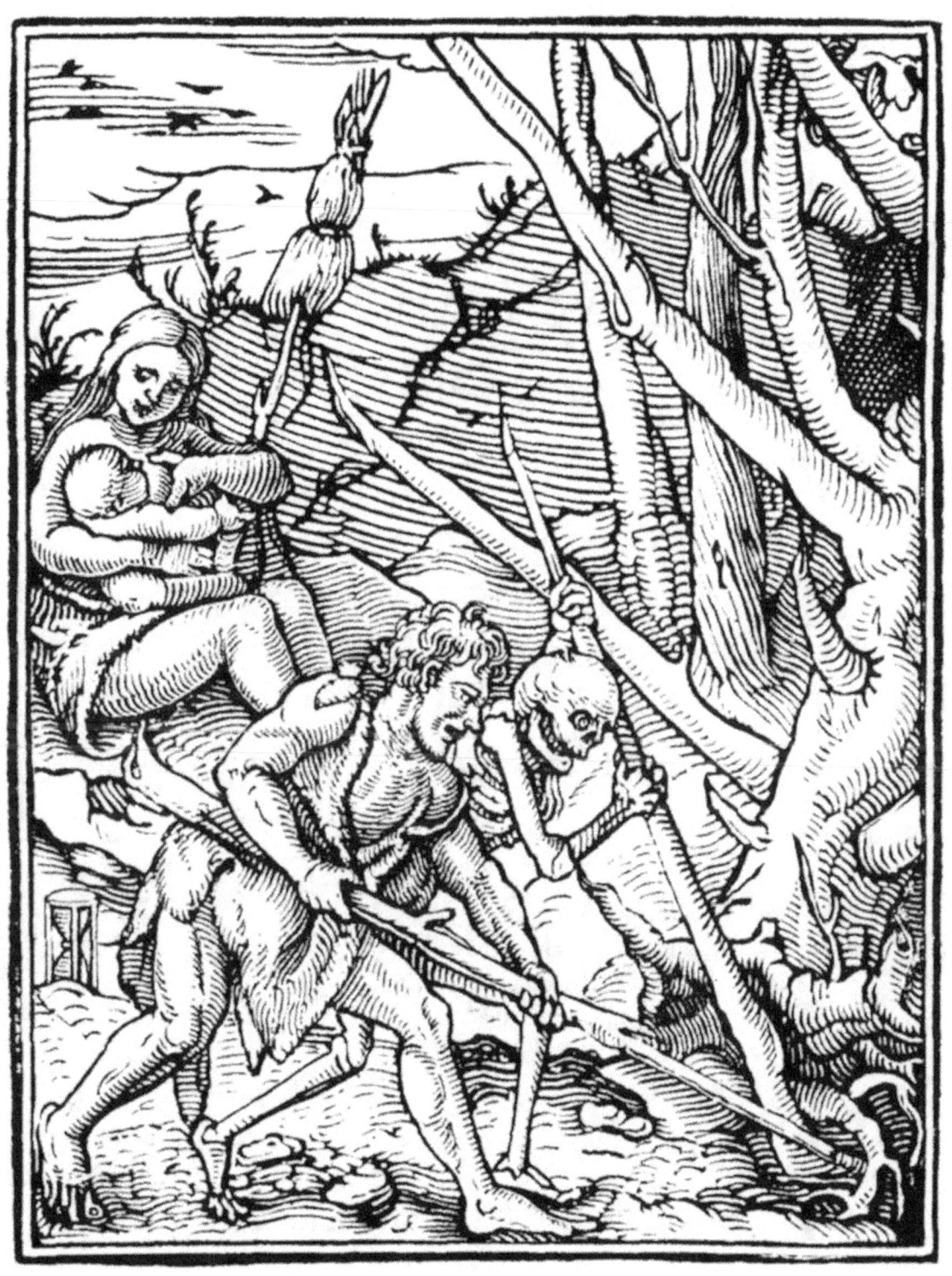

V

A CEMETERY

Gebein aller Menschen.

A crowd of skeletons, playing on horns, trumpets, and the like, summon mankind to the grave.

Woe! Woe! Woe! To the inhabiters of earth.

REVELATION 8:13

All in whose nostrils was the breath of life … died.

GENESIS 7:22

Woe! Woe! Inhabitants of Earth,
Where blighting cares so keenly strike,
And, spite of rank, or wealth, or worth,
Death—Death will visit all alike.

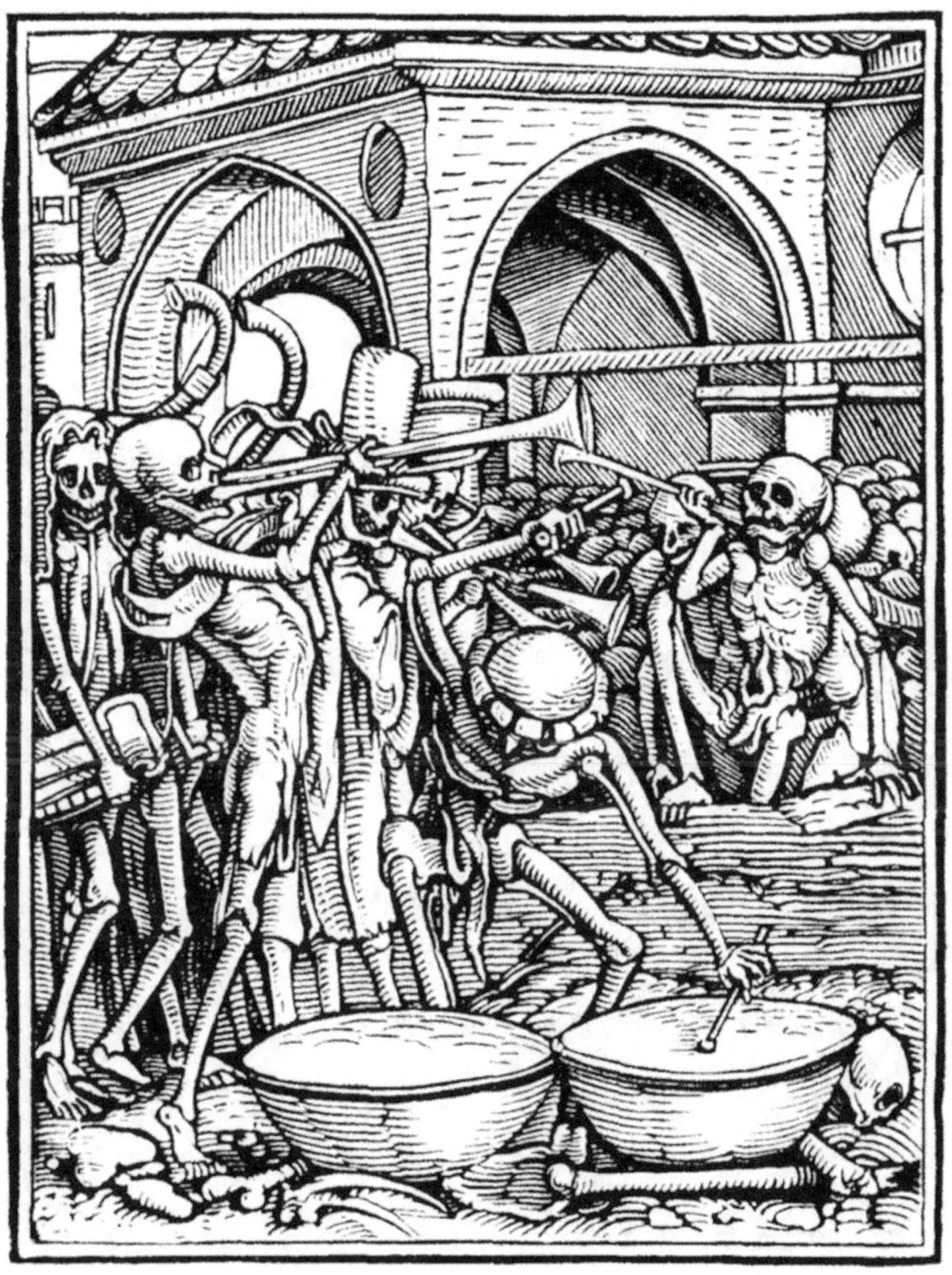

VI

THE POPE

Der Päpst.

The Pope (Leo X.) with Death at his side, crowns an Emperor, who kisses his foot. Another Death, in a cardinal's hat, is among the assistants.

Until the death of the high priest that shall be in those days.

JOSHUA 20:6

Let another take his office.

PSALM 109:8

Pride dreams an earthly immortality,
But Death is certain—sudden to destroy;
And even thou, high-priest, shalt surely die,
And a successor thy proud throne enjoy.

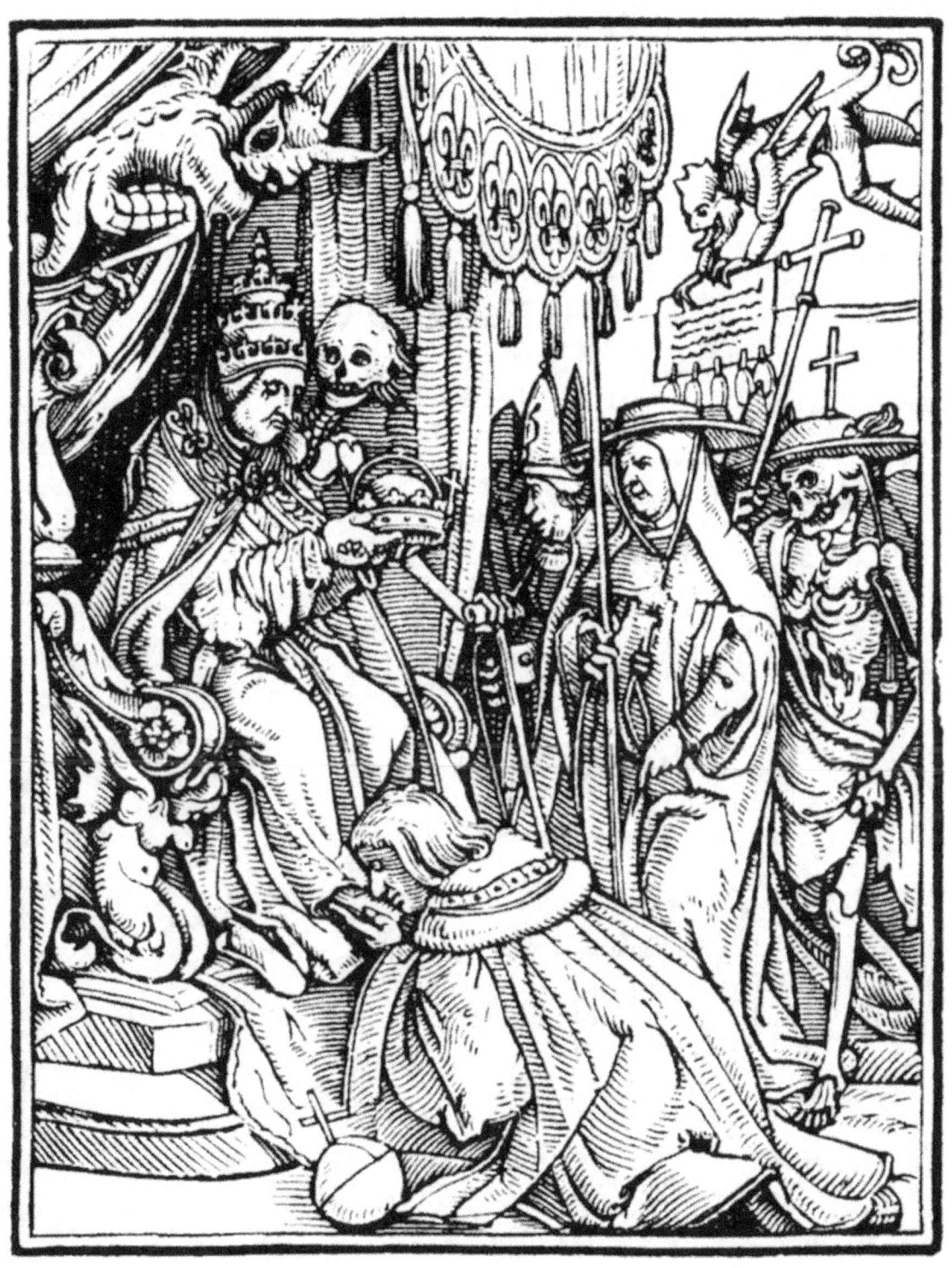

VII

⌇

THE EMPEROR

Der Kaiser.

The Emperor (Maximilian I.) rates his minister for injustice to a suitor. But even in the act Death discrowns him.

———

Set thine house in order: for thou shalt die, and not live.

Isaiah 38:1

There shalt thou die, and there the chariots of thy glory shall
be the shame of thy lord's house.

Isaiah 22:18

Order thine house while thou hast breath,
Bestow thy goods; for thou must die,
And soon within the realms of Death,
The chariots of thy state shall lie.

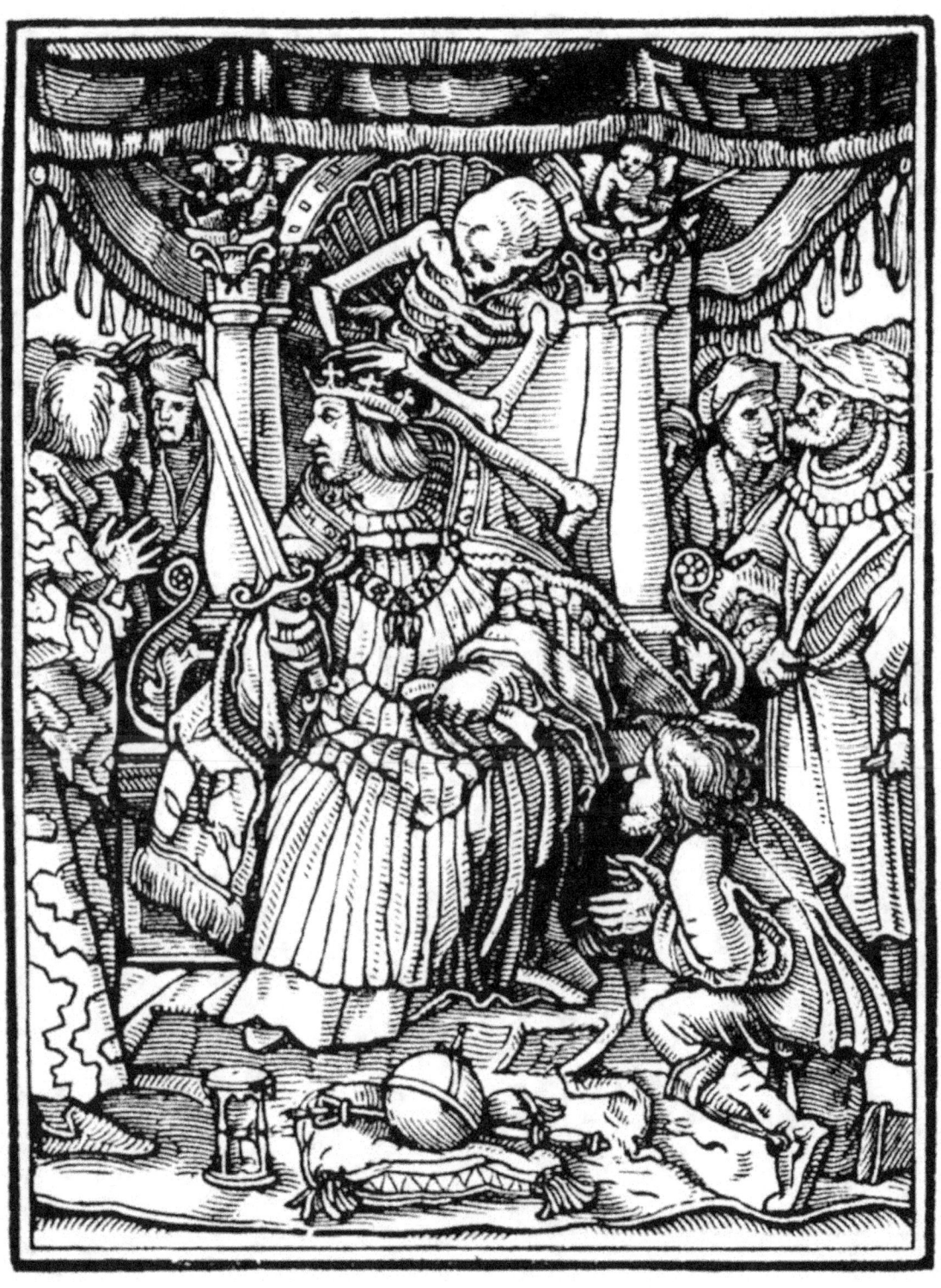

VIII

THE KING

Der König.

The King (Francis I.) sits at feast under a baldachin sprinkled with fleurs-de-lis. Death, as a cup-bearer, pours his last draught.

And he that is today a king, tomorrow shall die.

ECCLESIASTICUS 10:10

He who today is yet a king,
Tomorrow shall entombed be,
Nor carry with him anything,
Of all his transient royalty.

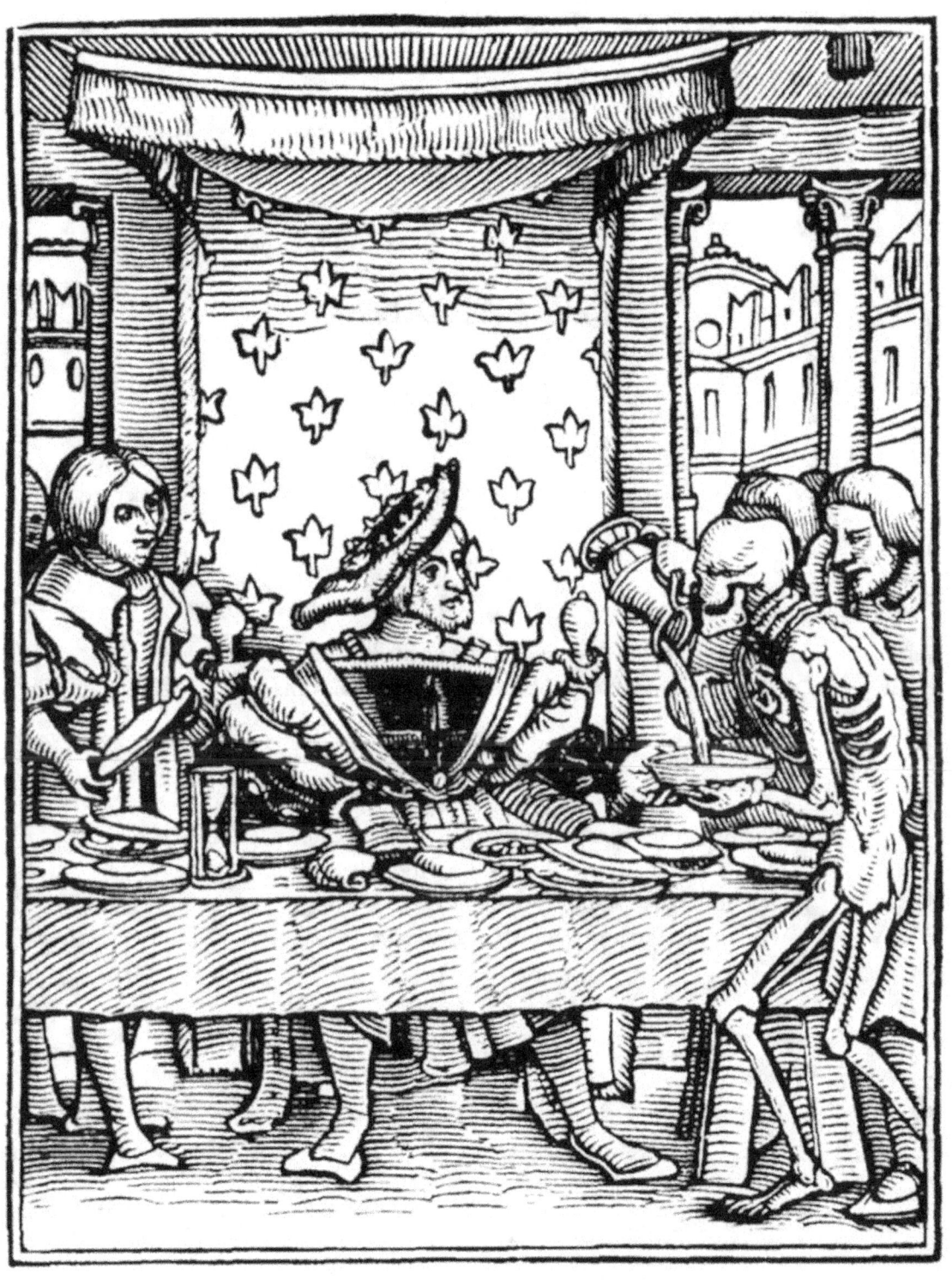

IX

❦

THE CARDINAL

Der Cardinal.

Death lifts off the Cardinal's hat as he is handing a letter of indulgence to a rich man. Luther's opponent, Cardinal Cajetan, is supposed to be represented.

Woe unto them which justify the wicked for reward, and take away the righteousness of the righteous from him.

ISAIAH 5:22 & 23

Woe unto ye, unjust, who justify
The wicked man, and shameful profit make,
Pretending his bad deeds to sanctify,
While from the just ye do all justice take.

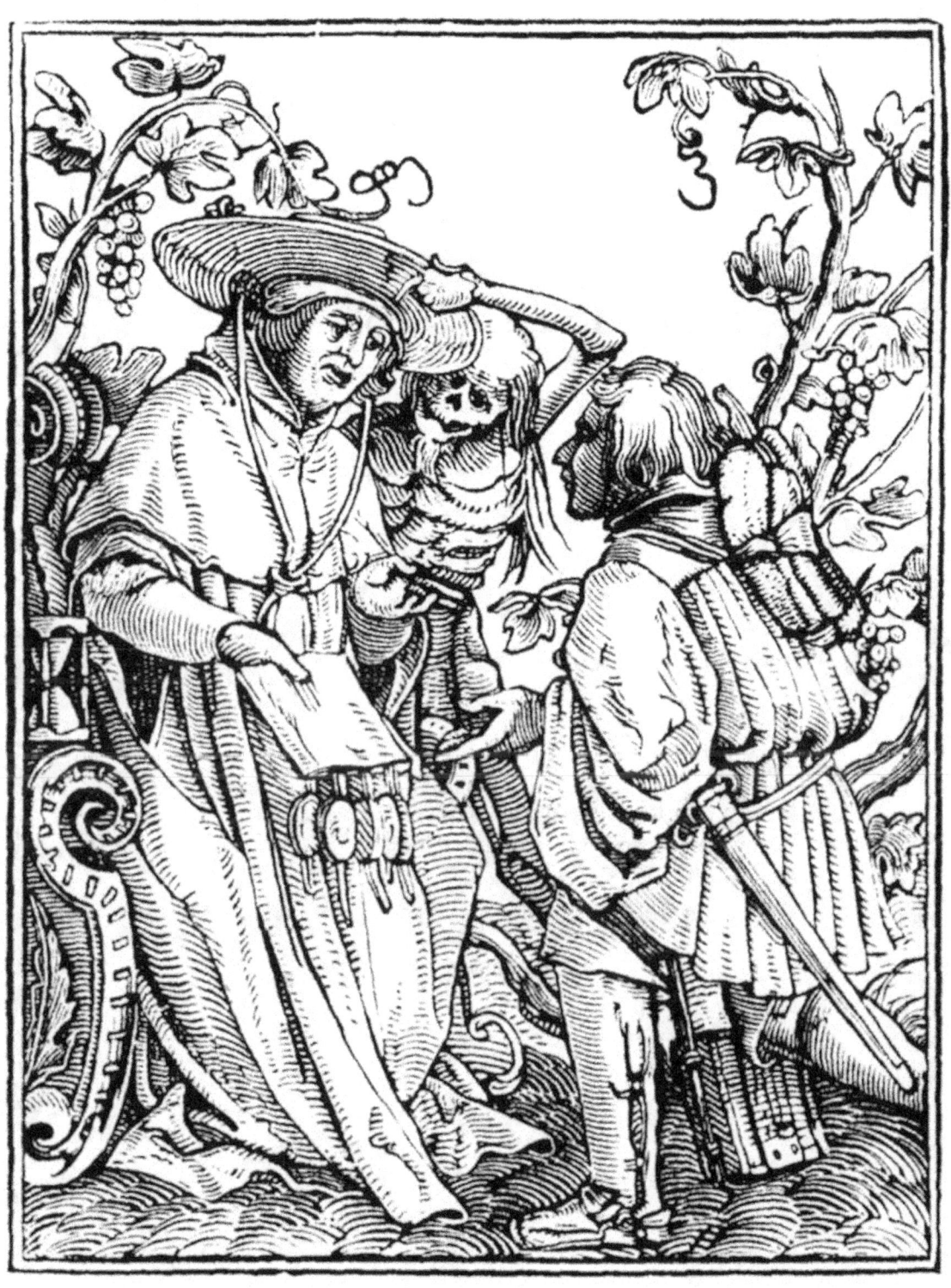

X

THE EMPRESS

Die Kaiserinn.

The Empress, walking with her women, is intercepted by a female Death, who conducts her to an open grave.

And those that walk in pride he is able to abase.

DANIEL 4:37

Ye who walk forth in pomp superb,
Within brief space to Death must bow;
As bends beneath the tread the herb,
Ye also must be trodden low.

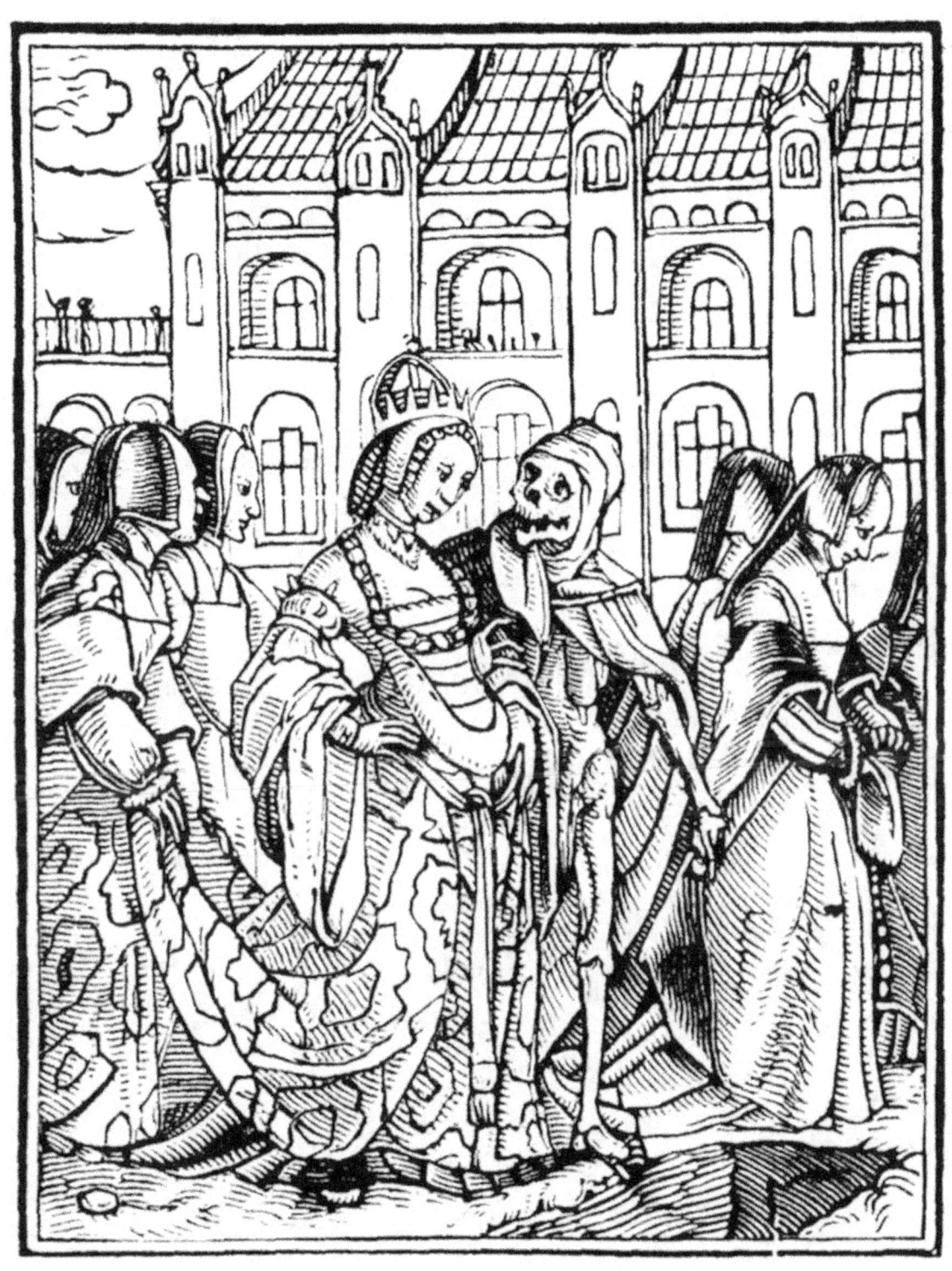

XI

THE QUEEN

Die Königinn.

Death, in the guise of a court-jester, drags away the Queen as she is leaving her palace.

Rise up, ye women that are at ease; hear my voice, ye careless daughters; give ear unto my speech. Many days and years shall ye be troubled.

ISAIAH 32:9 & 10

Daughters of rank and wealth, arise!
List to a warning from the dead;
After vain days and years misspent,
Come pangs that ye shall learn to dread.

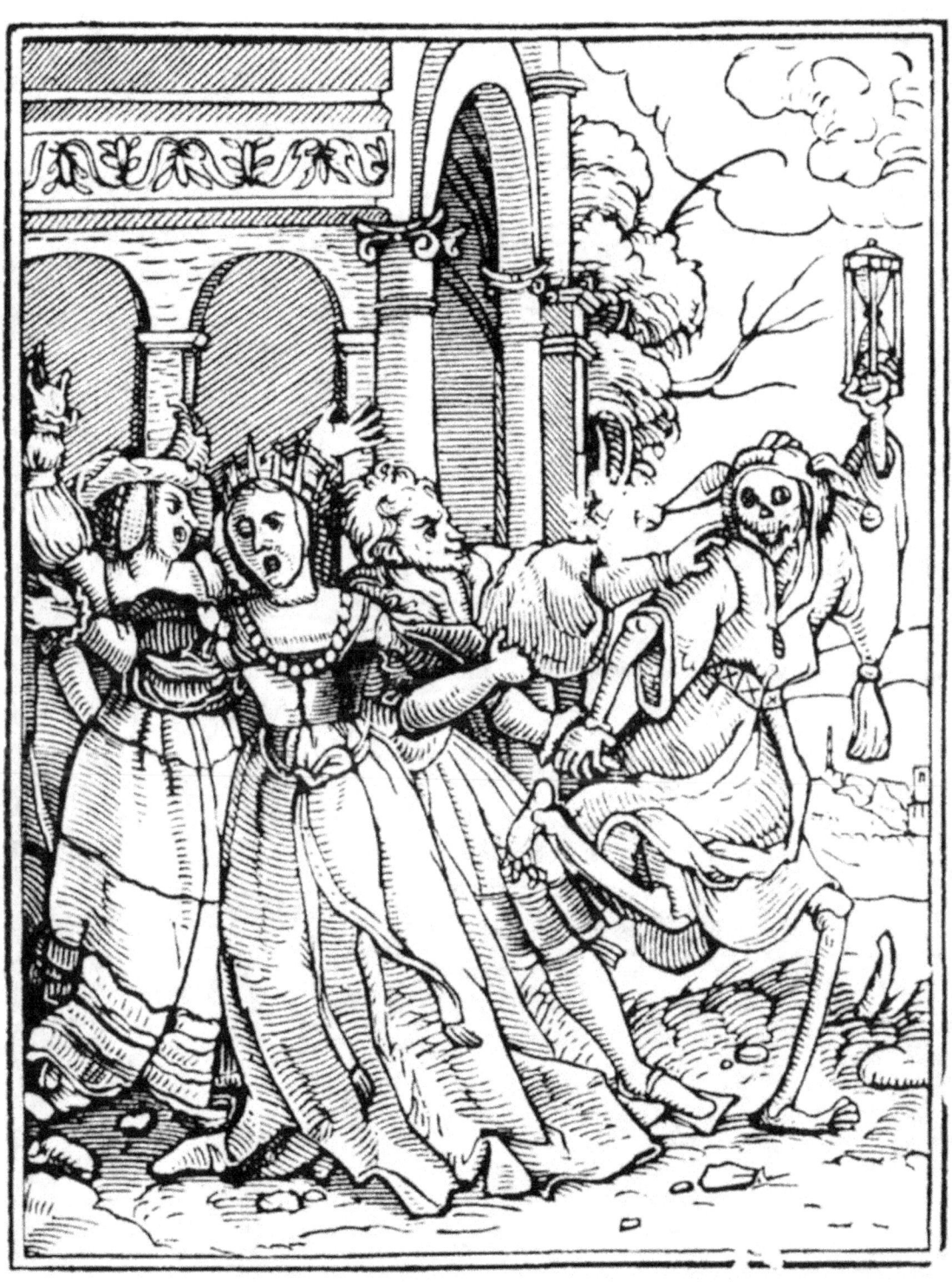

XII

—◆—

THE BISHOP

Der Bischof.

The sun is setting, and Death leads the aged Bishop from the sorrowing shepherds of his flock.

————◆————

I will smite the shepherd, and the sheep shall be scattered.

Mark 14:27

The pastor from his sheep I'll take;
Mitre and crosier cast to ground;
And when the shepherd I o'ertake,
The scatter'd flock shall scarce be found.

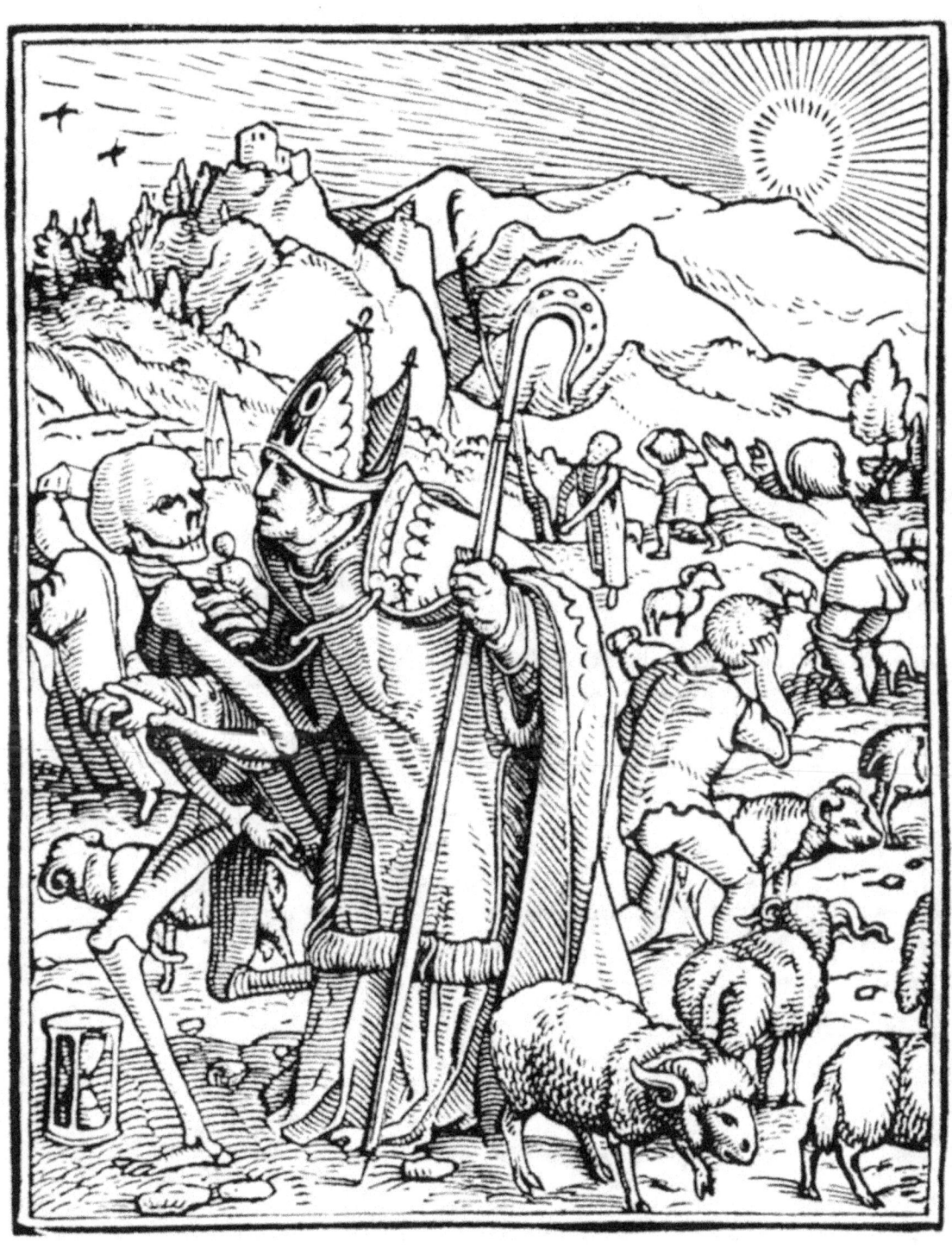

XIII

❦ ❦

THE DUKE

Der Herzog.

The Duke turns pitilessly from a beggar-woman and her child. Meanwhile Death, fantastically crowned, lays hands on him.

The prince shall be clothed in desolation … I will also make
the pomp of the strong to cease.

EZEKIEL 7:27 & 24

Come, potent prince, with me alone—
Leave transient pomps of worldly state;
I am the one who can fling down
The pride and honours of the great.

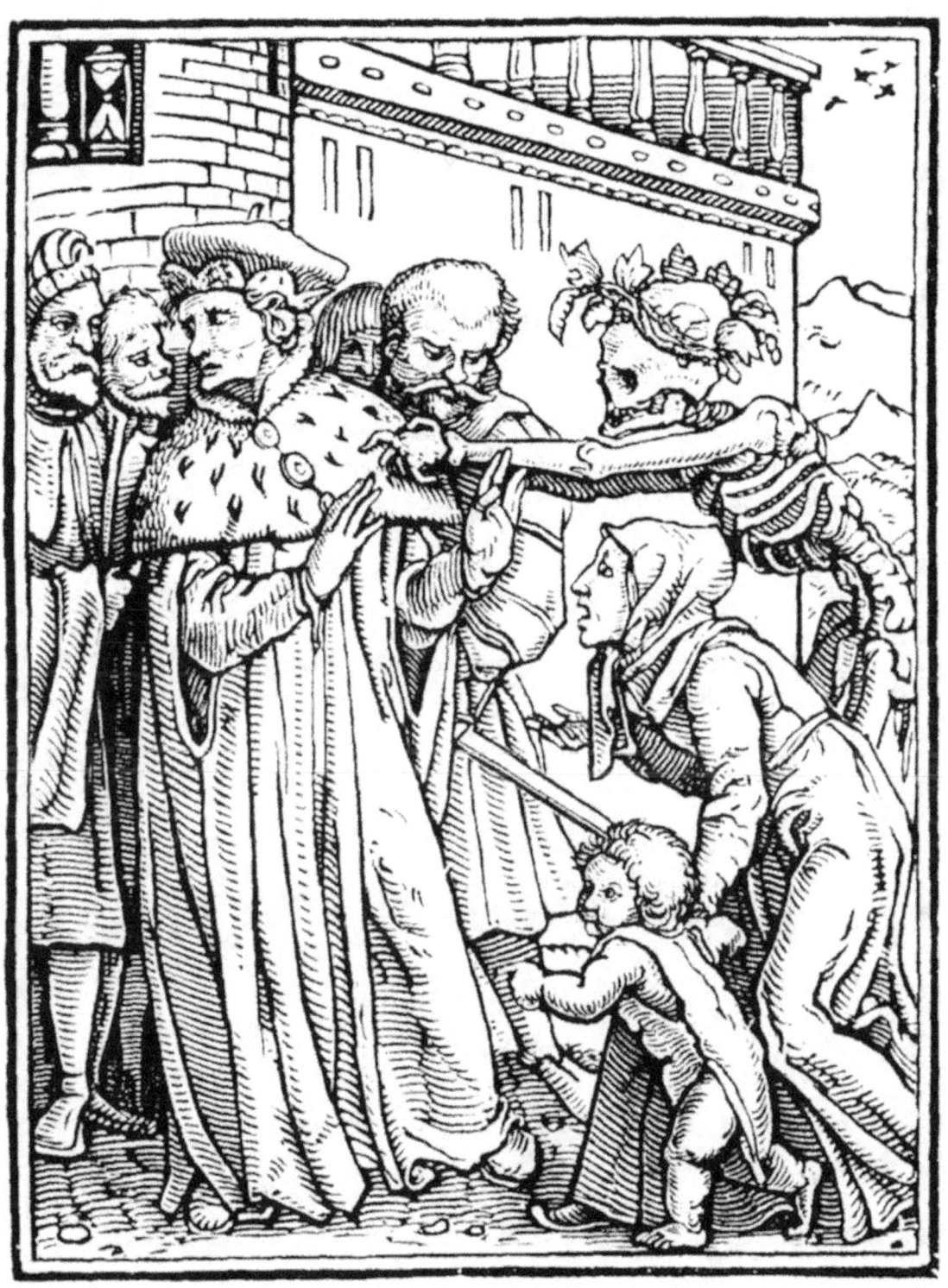

XIV

❧ ❧

THE ABBOT

Der Abt.

Death, having despoiled the Abbot of mitre and crozier, hales him along unwilling, and threatening his enemy with his breviary.

———

He shall die without instruction; and in the greatness of his folly shall he go astray.

PROVERBS 5:23

He dies, and he has never learned
The discipline that points the way
To the true life—while he has turned
To lusts that lead the soul astray.

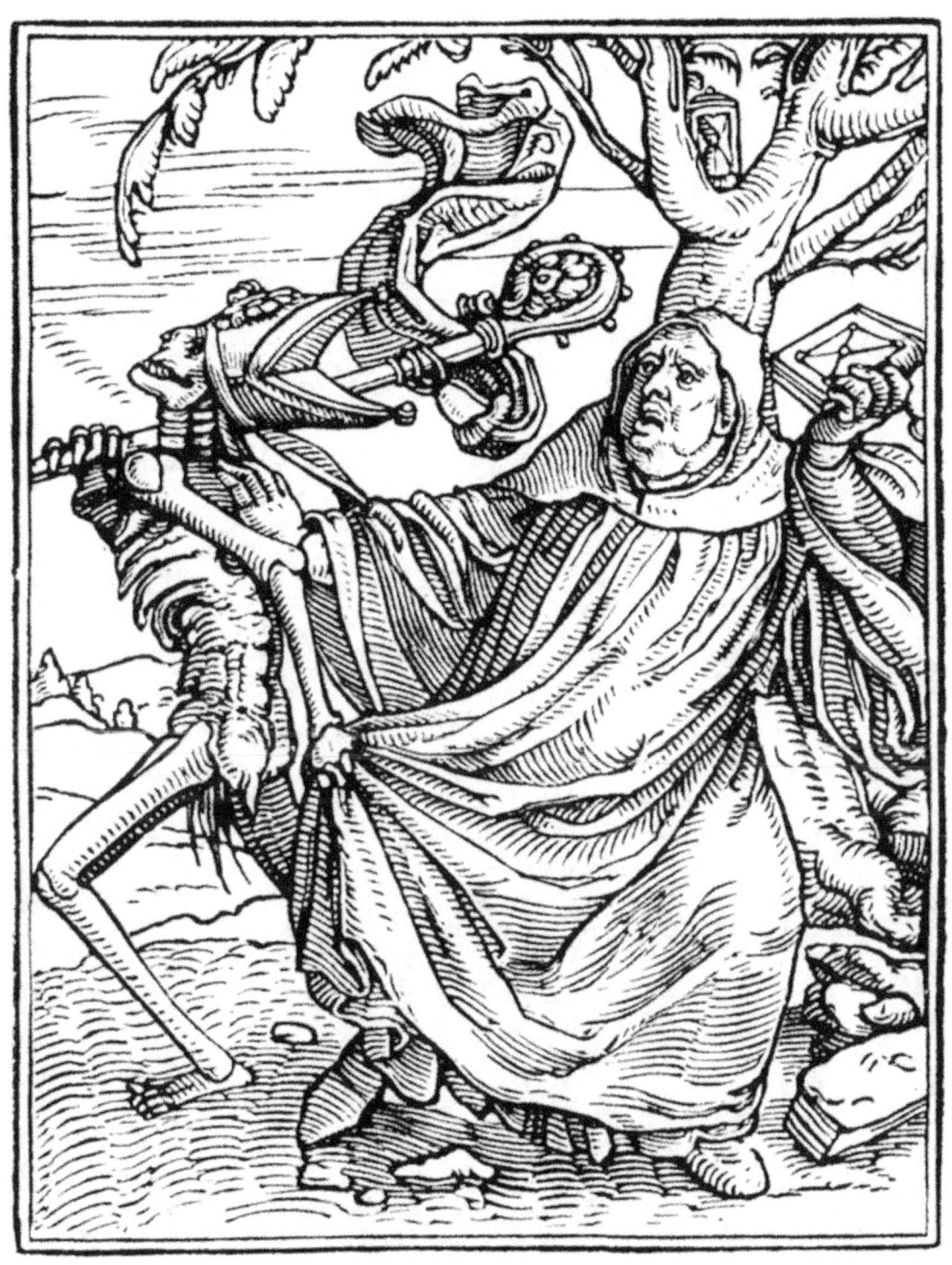

XV

❦ ❦

THE ABBESS

Die Abtissin.

Death, in a wreath of flags, pulls away the Abbess by her scapulary in sight of a shrieking nun.

—— • ◆ • ——

Wherefore I praised the dead which are already dead more
than the living which are yet alive.

ECCLESIASTES 4:2

The dead, she urged, I'm ever praising
More than the living, who in sin are found;
And yet, in Death's o-er-rude appraising,
I'm ranked with worldly sinners who abound.

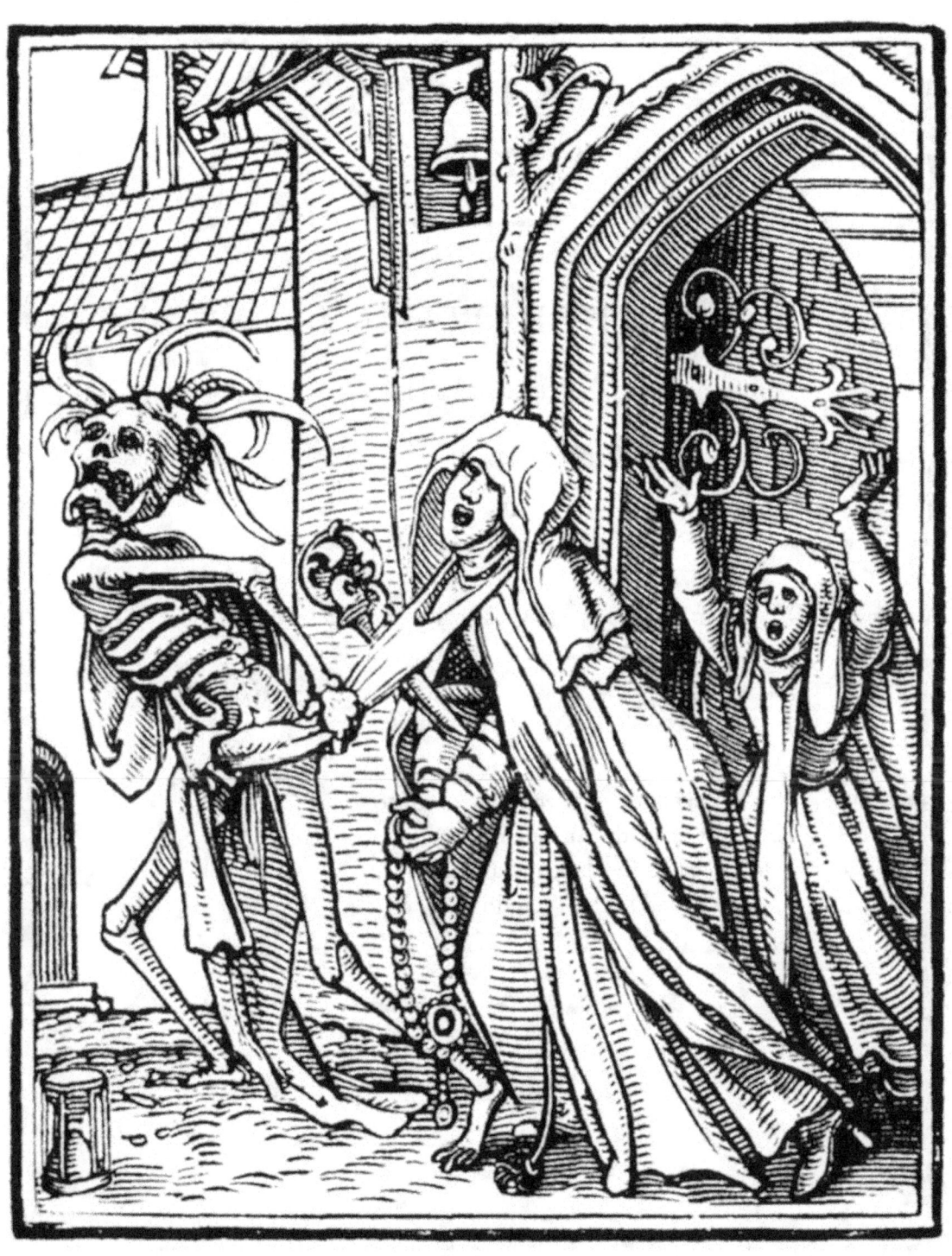

XVI

THE NOBLEMAN

Der Edelmann.

Death drags the resisting Nobleman towards a bier in the background.

What man is it that liveth, and shall not see Death? Shall he
deliver his soul from the hand of the grave?

PSALMS 89:48

Who is the man, however strong or great,
Who can escape the final destiny?—
Who can avoid the dark and awful gate,
Or cheat grim Death of certain victory?

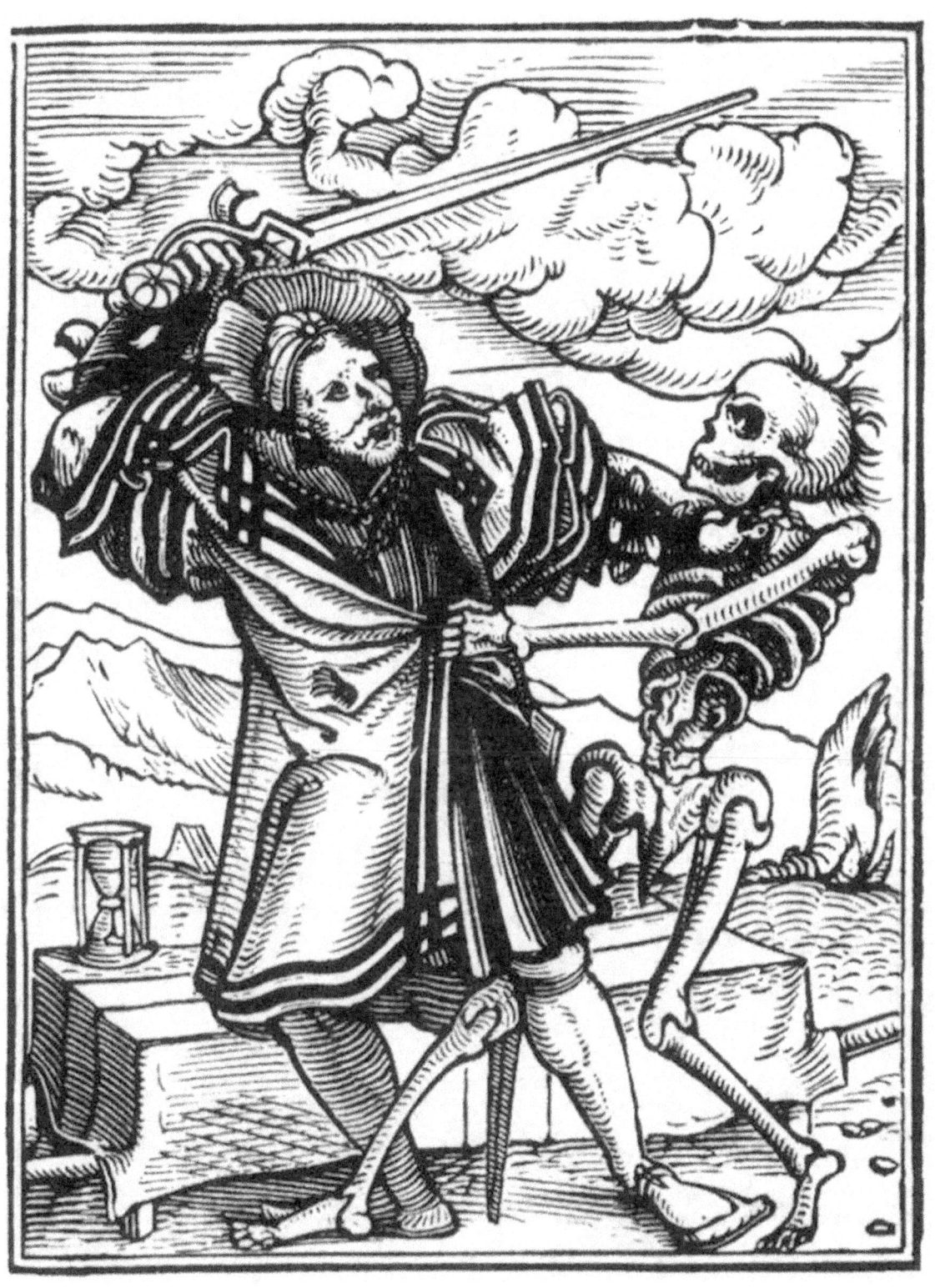

XVII

THE CANON, OR PREBENDARY

Der Domherr.

The Canon, with his falconer, page, and jester, enters the church door. Death shows him that his sands have run.

Behold, the hour is at hand.

MATTHEW 26:45

In choir each day thou mutterest prayer;
Today that muttering may not be;
Thou must e'en die—all unaware,
Behold! 't is time; so come to me!

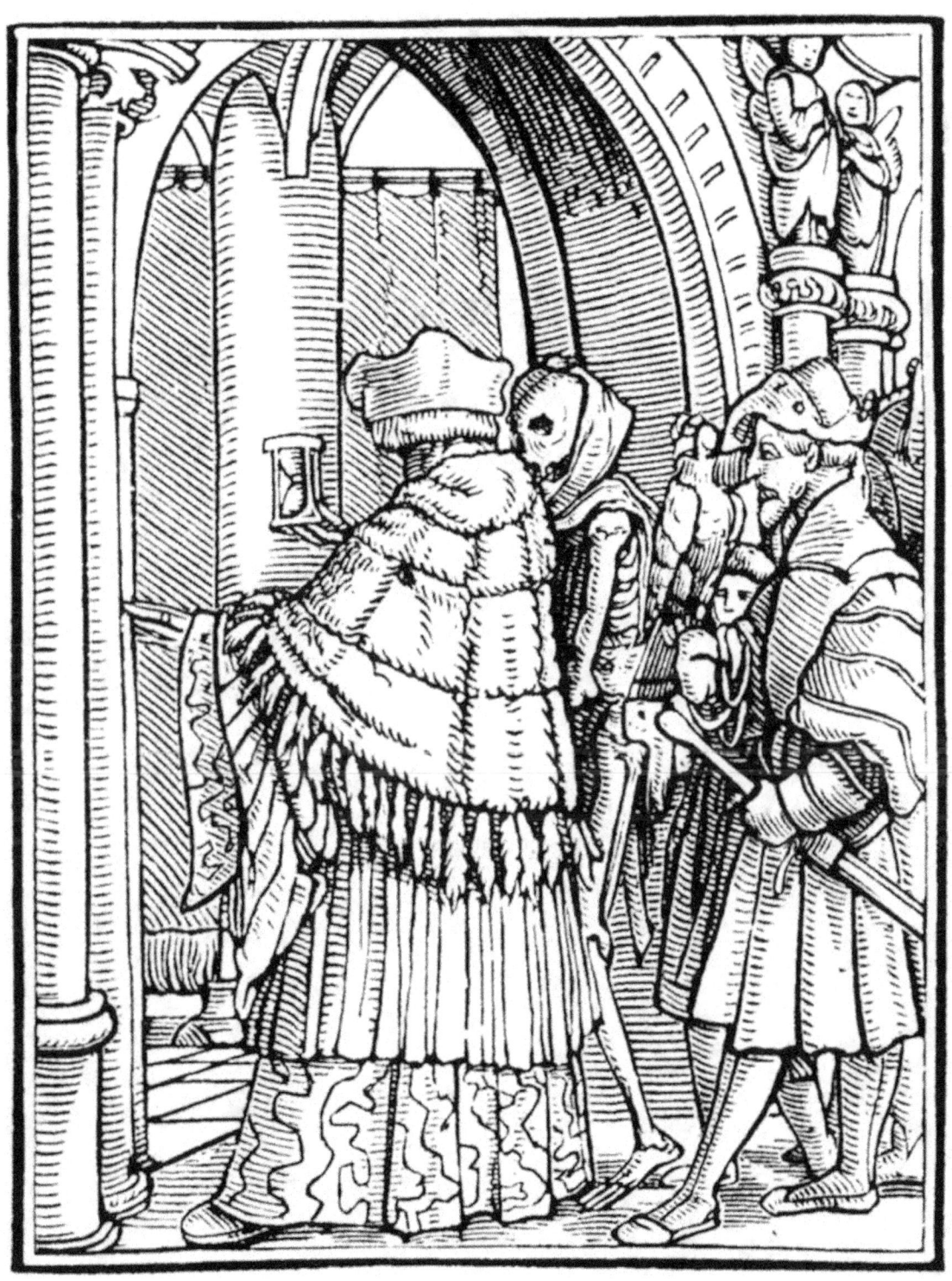

XVIII

—◆—

THE JUDGE

Der Richter.

Death withdraws the Judge's staff as he takes a bribe from a rich suitor.

———◆———

And I will cut off the Judge from the midst thereof.

Amos 2:3

From out thy seat thou shalt be taken,
So oft bribed to iniquity—
Thy ill-got gains must be forgotten;
No bribe can buy thy life of me.

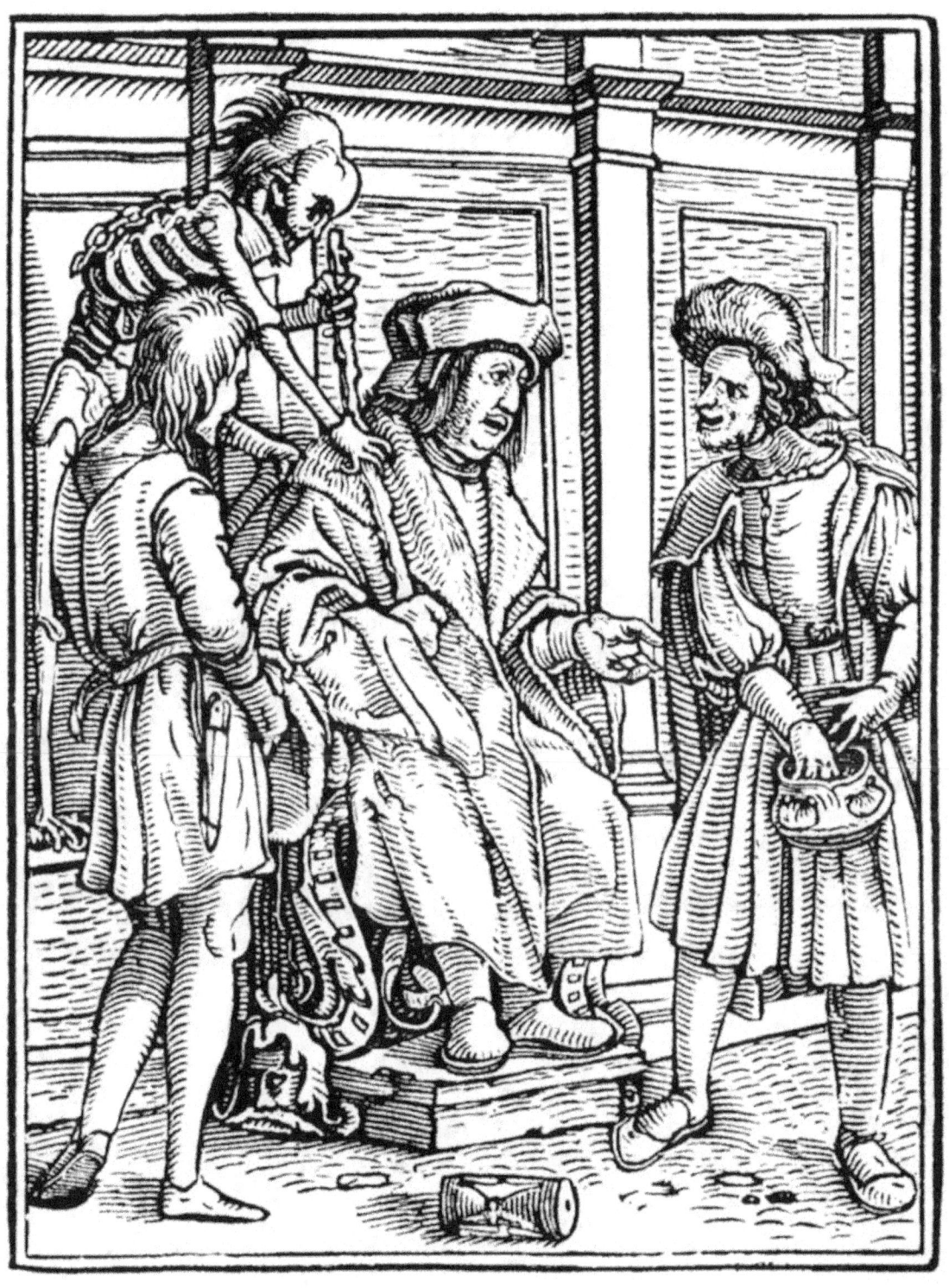

XIX

—◦—

THE ADVOCATE

Der Fürsprach.

Death comes upon him in the street while he is being feed by a rich client.

—◦◦◦—

A prudent man foreseeth the evil, and hideth himself; but the
simple pass on, and are punished.

PROVERBS 22:3

The cautious man, with malice ever keen,
The simpler in his grasp will tightly bind
By legal cunning, and has ever been
The hard oppressor of his poorer kind.

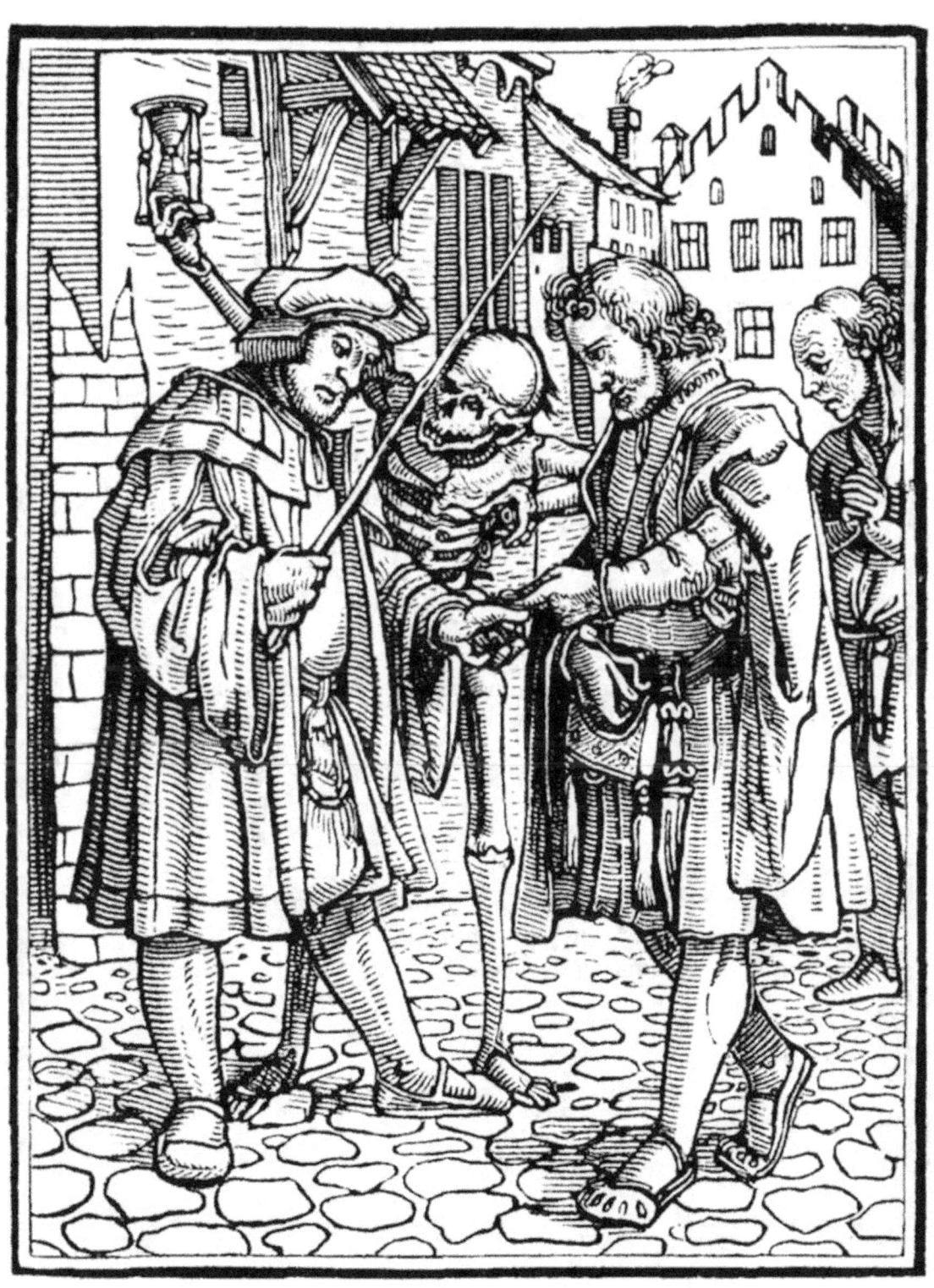

XX

⸺

THE COUNSELLOR, OR SENATOR

Der Rathsherr.

The Counsellor, prompted by a devil, is absorbed by a nobleman, and turns unheeding from a poor suppliant. But Death, with glass and spade, is waiting at his feet.

⸺

Whoso stoppeth his ears at the cry of the poor, he also shall cry himself, but shall not be heard.

Proverbs 21:13

Ye rich, who cautious counsel take on gain,
Ye cannot hear the starving poor man sue;
But, at the last, ye too will cry in vain,
And God will turn as deaf an ear to you.

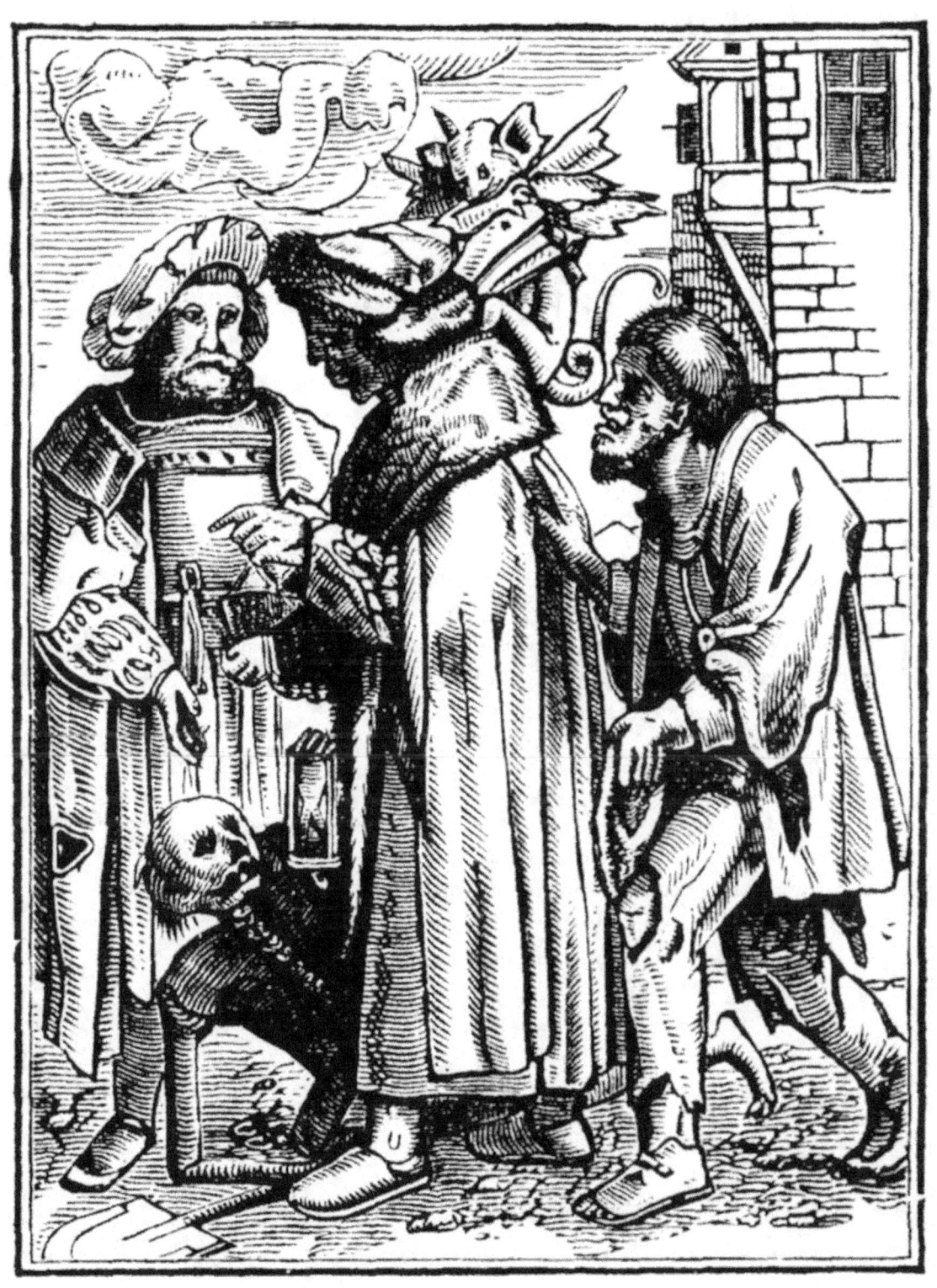

XXI

❧ ❧

THE PREACHER

Der Predicant.

Death, in a stole, stands in the pulpit behind the fluent Preacher, and prepares to strike him down with a jaw-bone.

———————

Woe unto them that call evil good, and good evil; that put darkness for light, and light for darkness; that put bitter for sweet, and sweet for bitter.

ISAIAH 5:20

Woe unto ye who do so profanely dare
Evil for good show, by praise or blame;
And, also, good things evil ones declare,
And sweet for bitter falsely do proclaim.

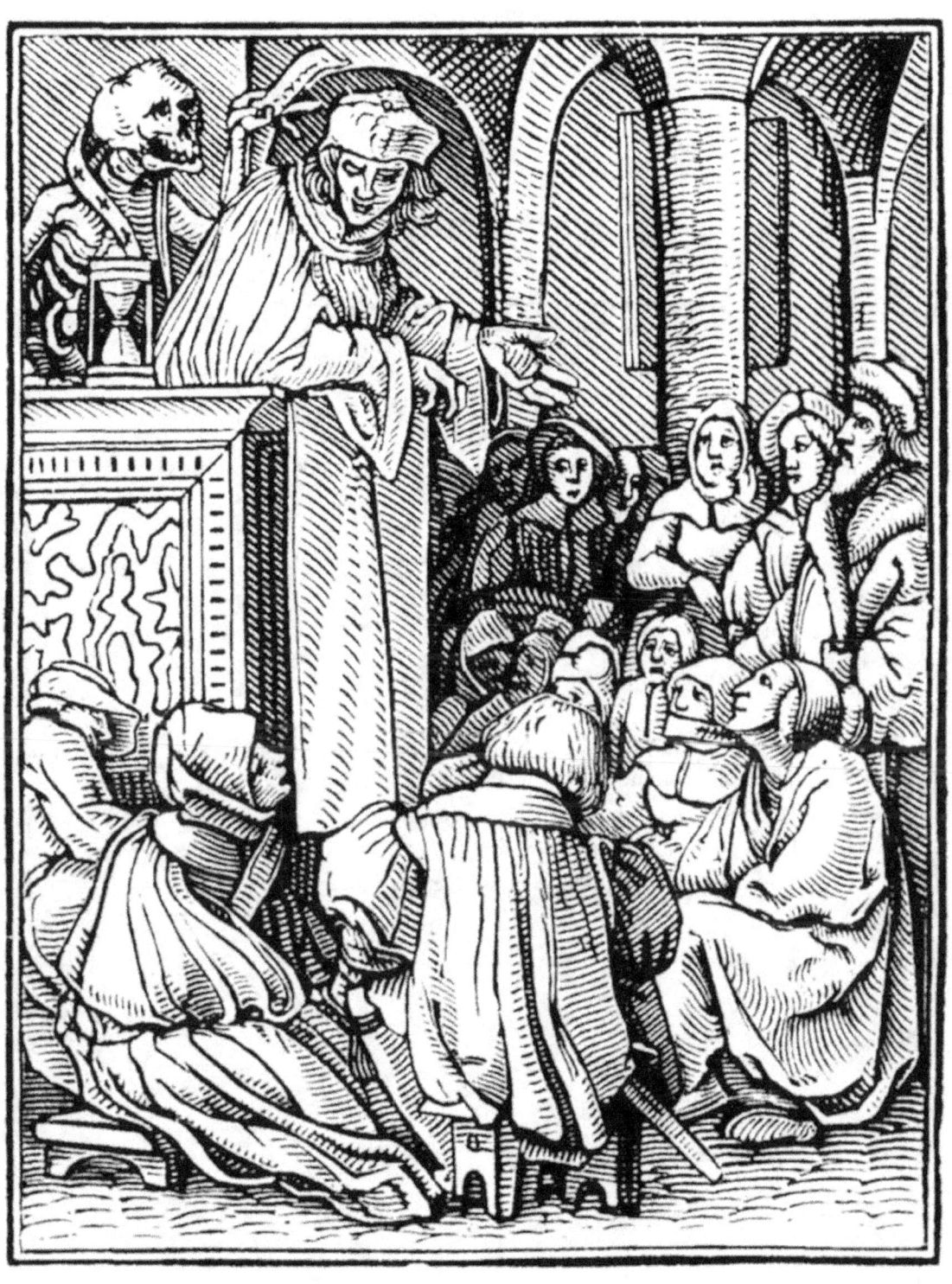

XXII

❦

THE PRIEST, OR PASTOR

Der Pfarrherr.

He carries the host to a sick person. But Death precedes him as his sacristan.

I myself also am a mortal man, like to all.

WISDOM OF SOLOMON 7:1

The holy sacrament I bear with me
To soothe the sinner in his last hour,
I, who am mortal too, as well as he,
And can no more than he evade Death's power.

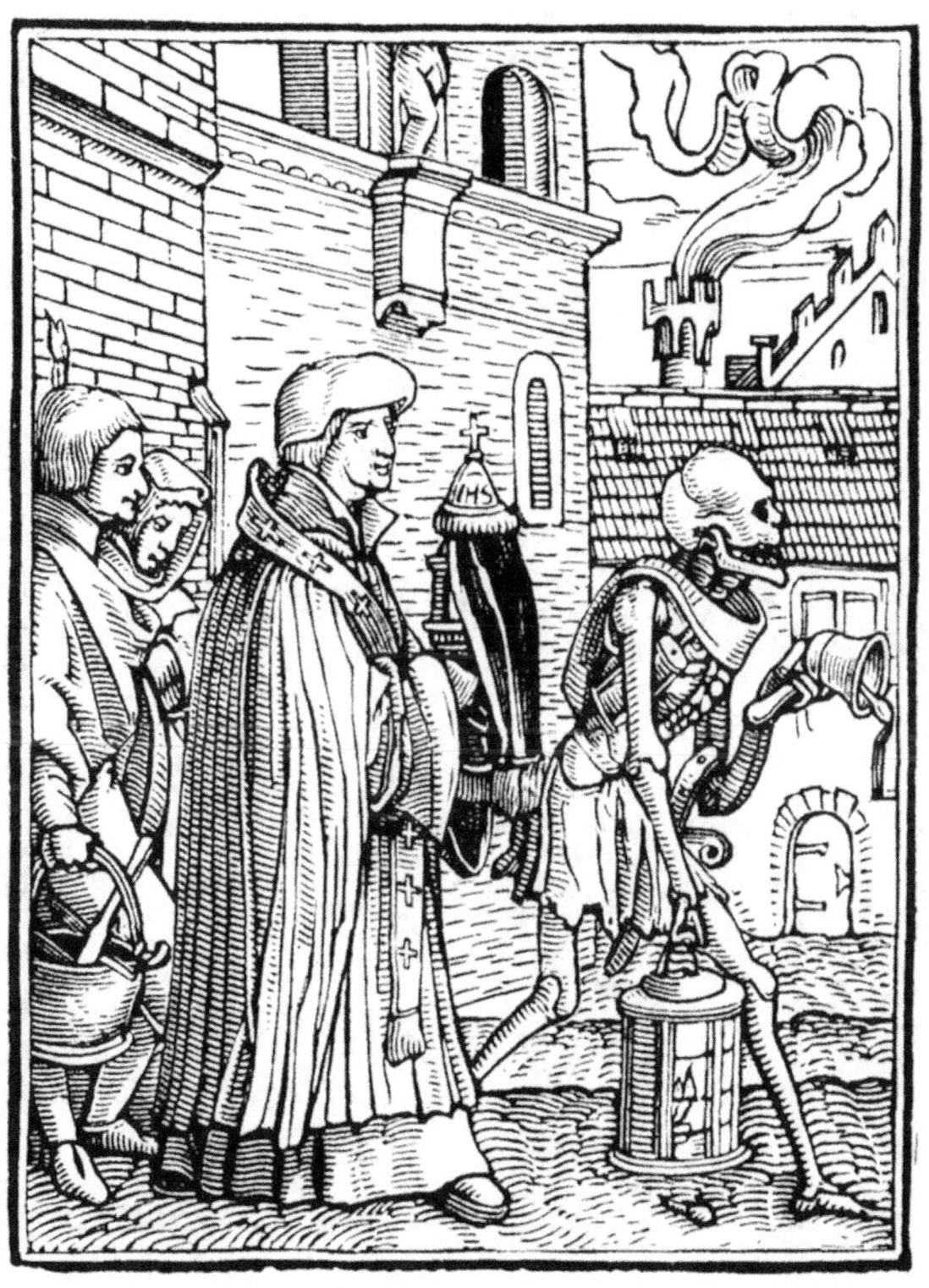

XXIII

THE MENDICANT FRIAR

Der Mönch.

Death seizes him just as his begging box and bag are filled.

Such as sit in darkness and in the shadow of death, being
bound in affliction.

PSALM 107:10

Thou who hast never felt remorse nor care,
Beyond the craft of thy mendacity,
Within the shadow of death I now will bear,
To save thee from such base necessity.

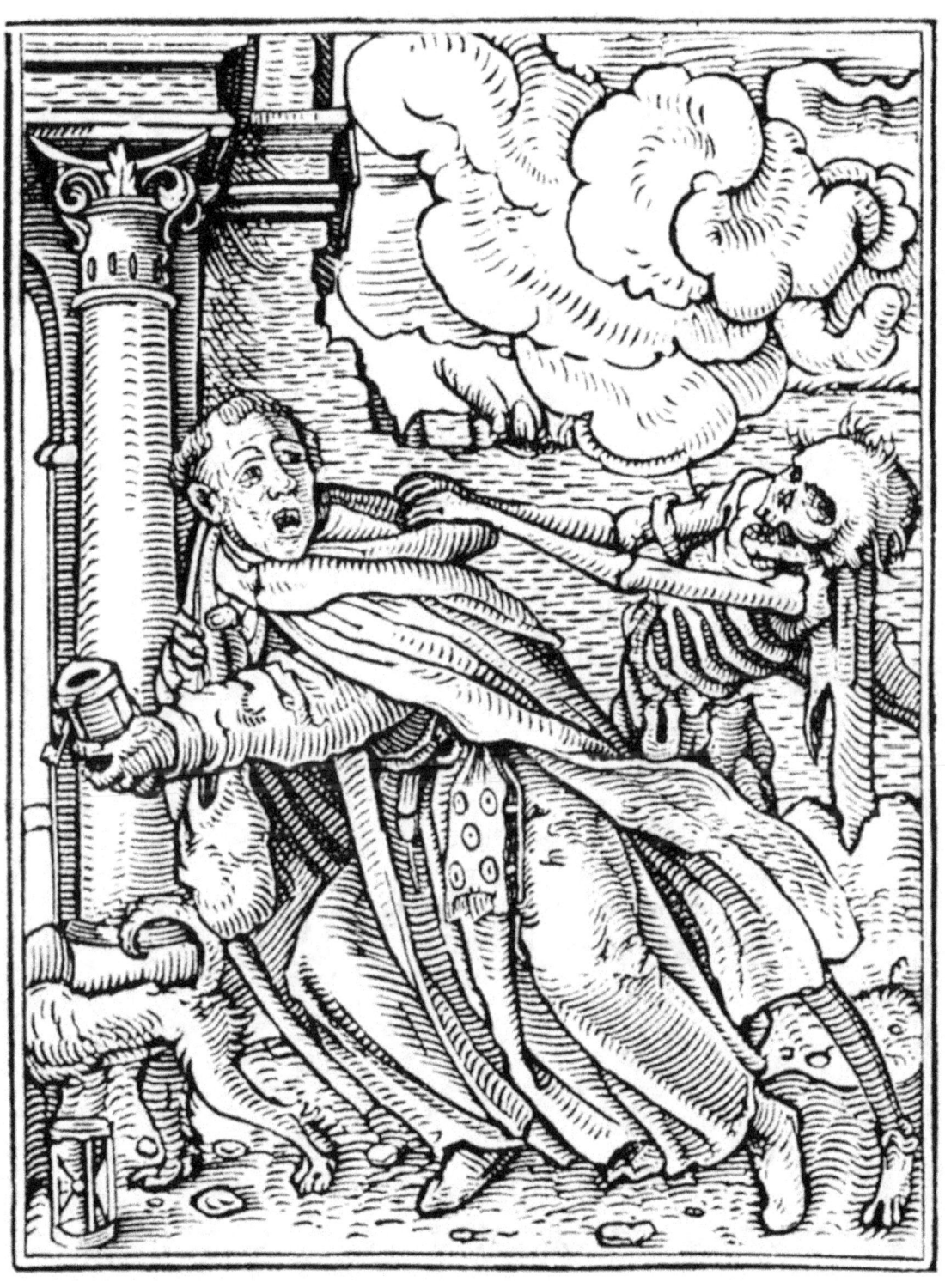

XXIV

THE NUN

Die Nonne.

The young Nun kneels at the altar, but turns to her lover who plays upon a lute. Death meantime, as a hideous old hag, extinguishes the altar candles.

———

There is a way which seemeth right unto a man; but the end thereof are the ways of death.

PROVERBS 14:12

Ill ways to human ken seem right,
Frail pleasures neither bad nor vain;
But Death they bring, with fatal blight,
Who yokes all sinners in his train.

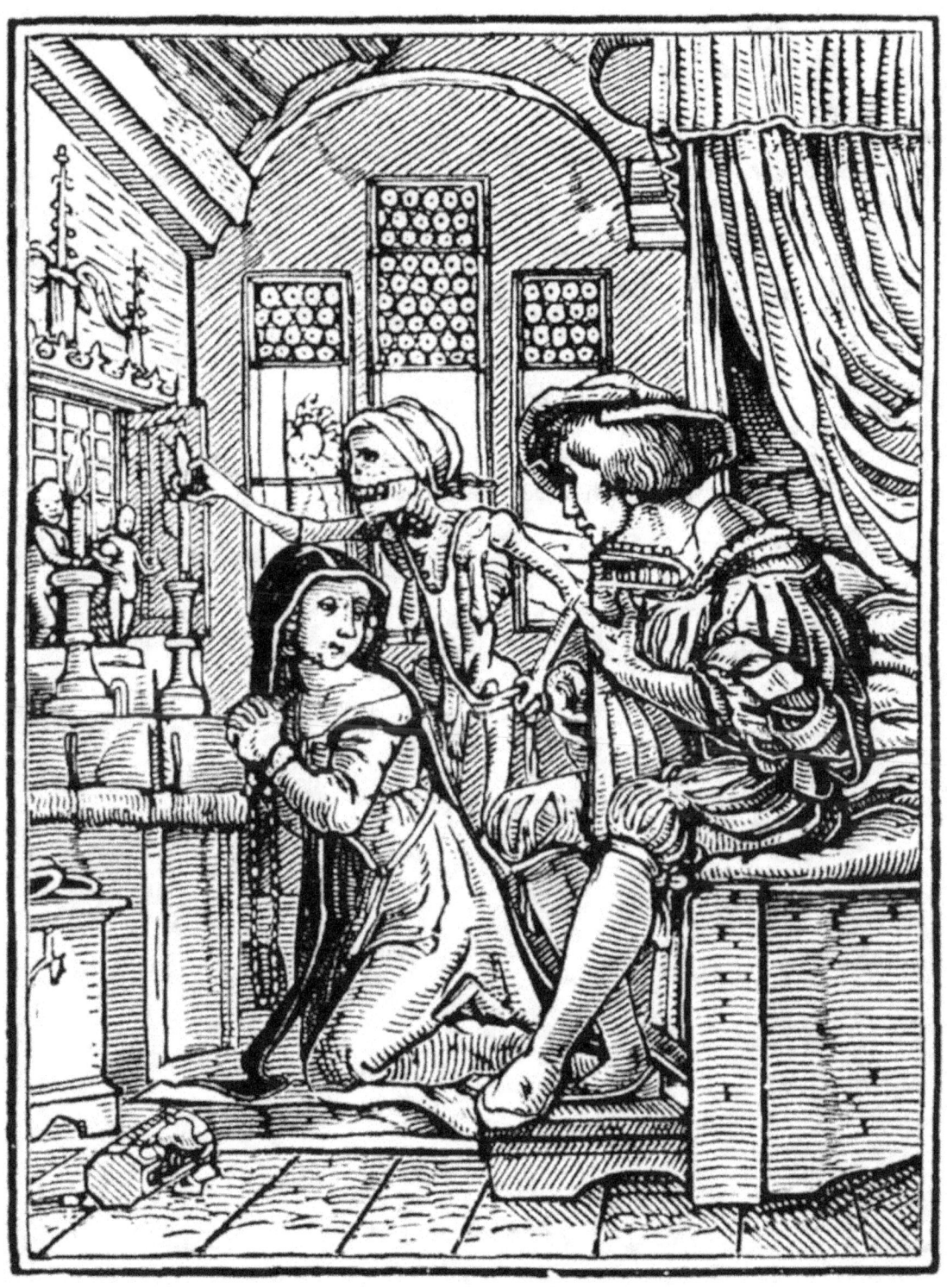

XXV

THE OLD WOMAN

Das Altweib.

"Melior est mors quam vita" to the aged woman who crawls gravewards with her bone rosary while Death makes music in the van.

Death is better than a bitter life or continued sickness.

ECCLESIATICUS 30:17

The love of life has ceased in thee,
Who long hast known this suffering strife;
Then come along to rest with me,
For Death is better now than life.

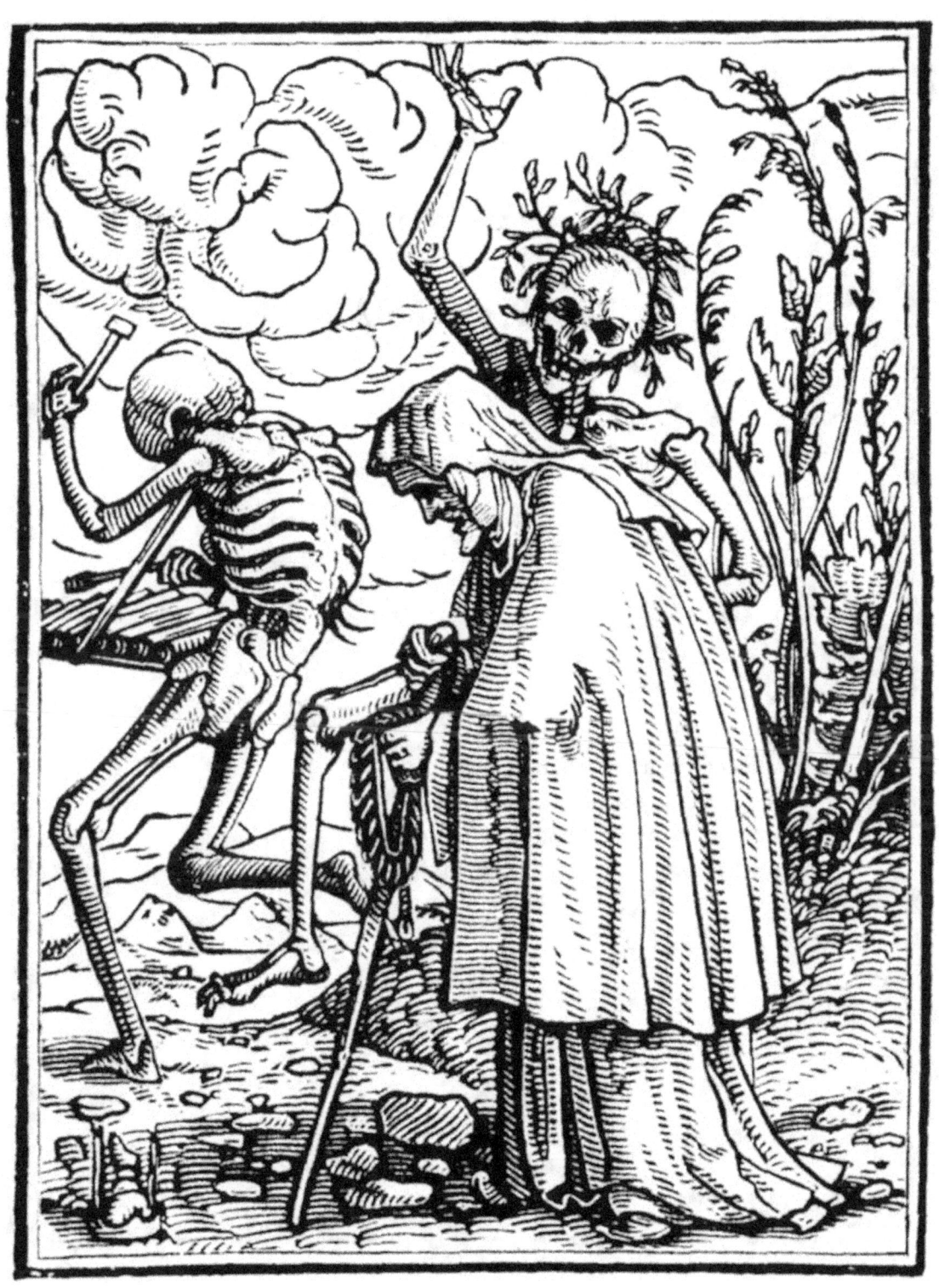

XXVI

—◆—

THE PHYSICIAN

Der Arzt.

Death brings him a hopeless patient, and bids him cure himself.

———◆◆◆———

Physician, heal thyself.

LUKE 4:23

Ailments thou understandest well,
And healer of the sick canst be;
But rash, vain man, thou canst not tell
In what form Death shall come to thee.

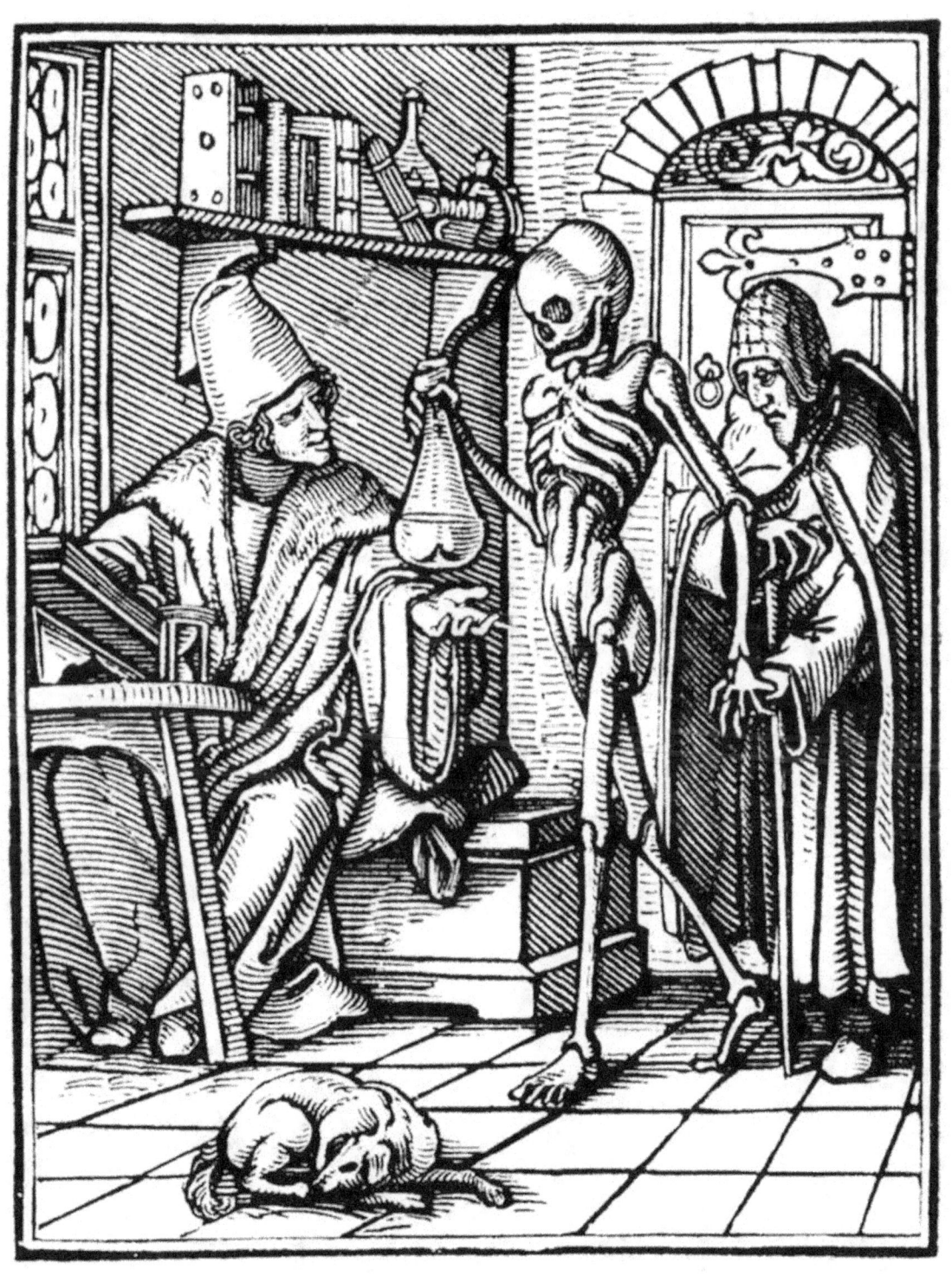

XXVII

THE ASTROLOGER

He contemplates a pendent sphere. But Death thrusts a skull before his eyes.

Knowest thou it because thou wast then born? Or because the
number of thy days is great?

JOB 38:21

Thou tell'st by amphibology
That which to others shall befall,
Then tell me by astrology
When thou shalt answer to my call.

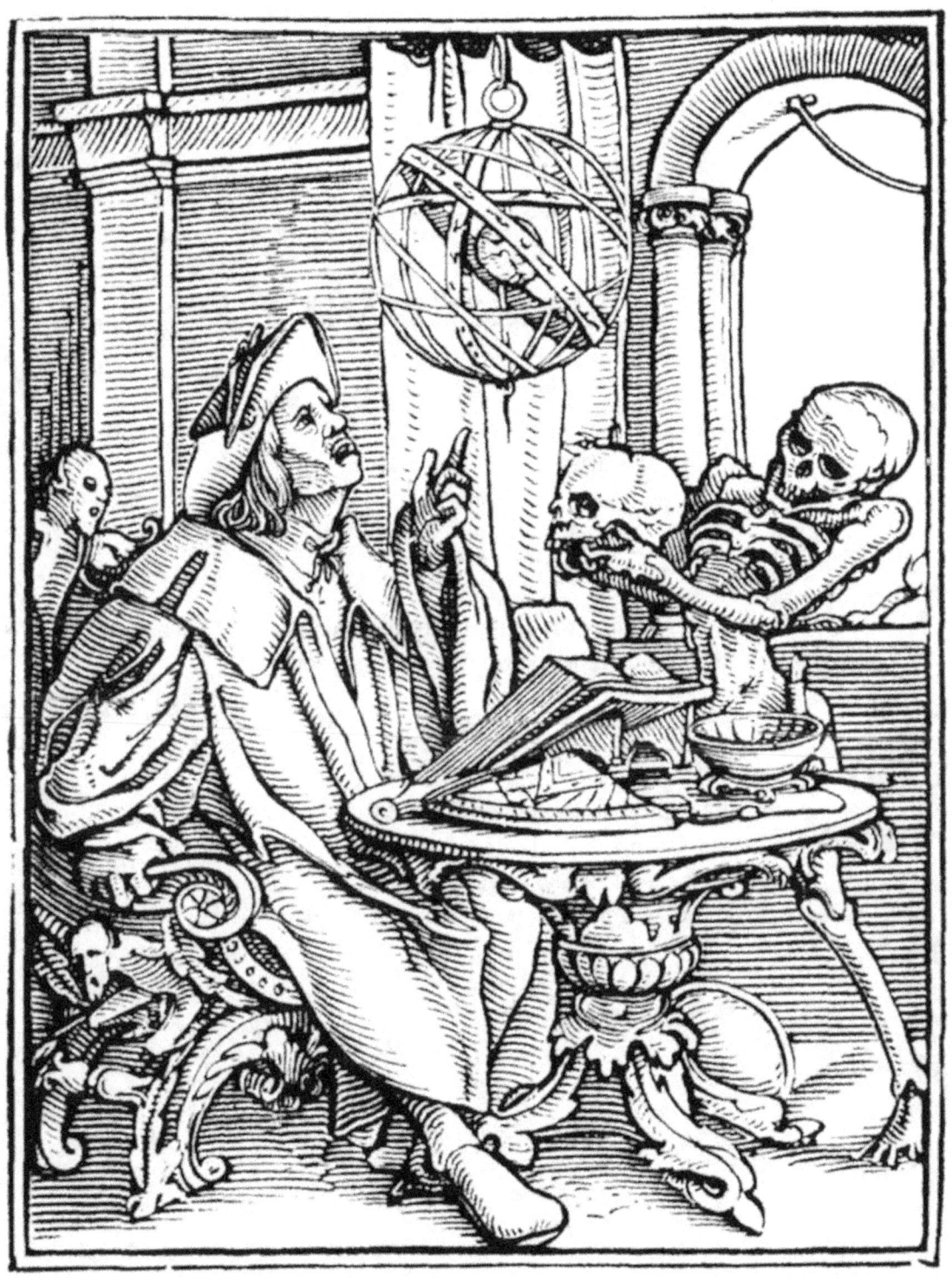

XXVIII

THE RICH MAN

Der Reichmann.

Death finds him at his pay-table and seizes the money.

Thou fool, this night thy soul shall be required of thee; then
whose shall those things be which thou hast provided?

LUKE 12:20

This very night shalt thou know Death!
Tomorrow be encoffined fast!
Then tell me, fool! While thou hast breath,
Who'll have the gold thou hast amassed?

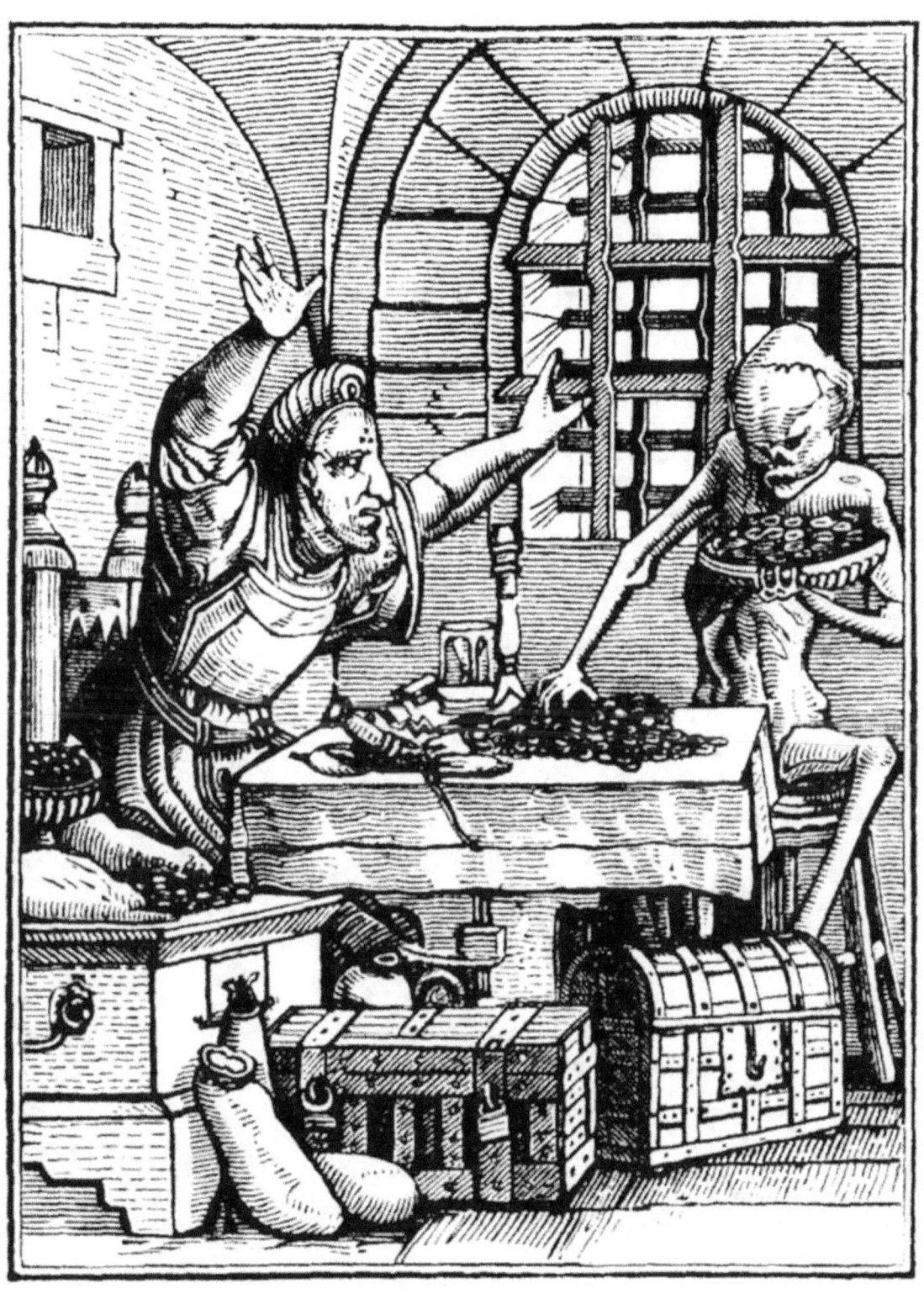

XXIX

~ · ~

THE MERCHANT

Der Kaufmann.

Death arrests him among his newly-arrived bales.

This getting of treasures by a lying tongue is a vanity tossed to
and fro of them that seek death.

PROVERBS 21:6

The Merchant's wealth's a worthless thing,
Of others, worn by lies, the spoils;
But Death will sure repentance bring,
Snaring the snarer in his toils.

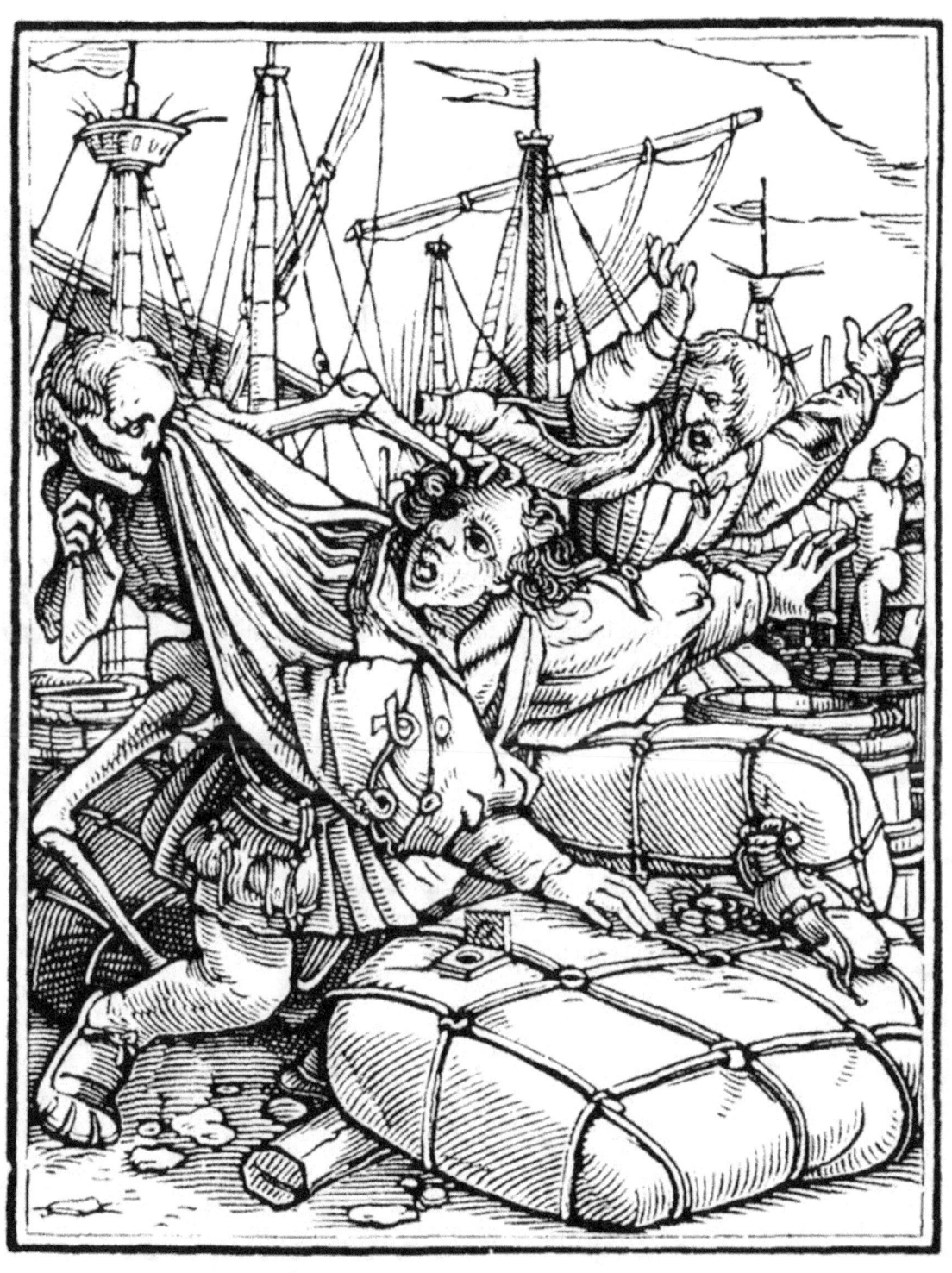

XXX

THE SHIPMAN

Der Schiffmann.

Death breaks the mast of the ship, and the crew are in extremity.

But they that will be rich fall into temptation and a snare,
and into many foolish and hurtful lusts, which drown men in
destruction and perdition.

I TIMOTHY 6:9

To gain the good things of this world,
What risks are dared without condition,
Seas braved! And treacherous sails unfurl'd!
So men rush on to their perdition.

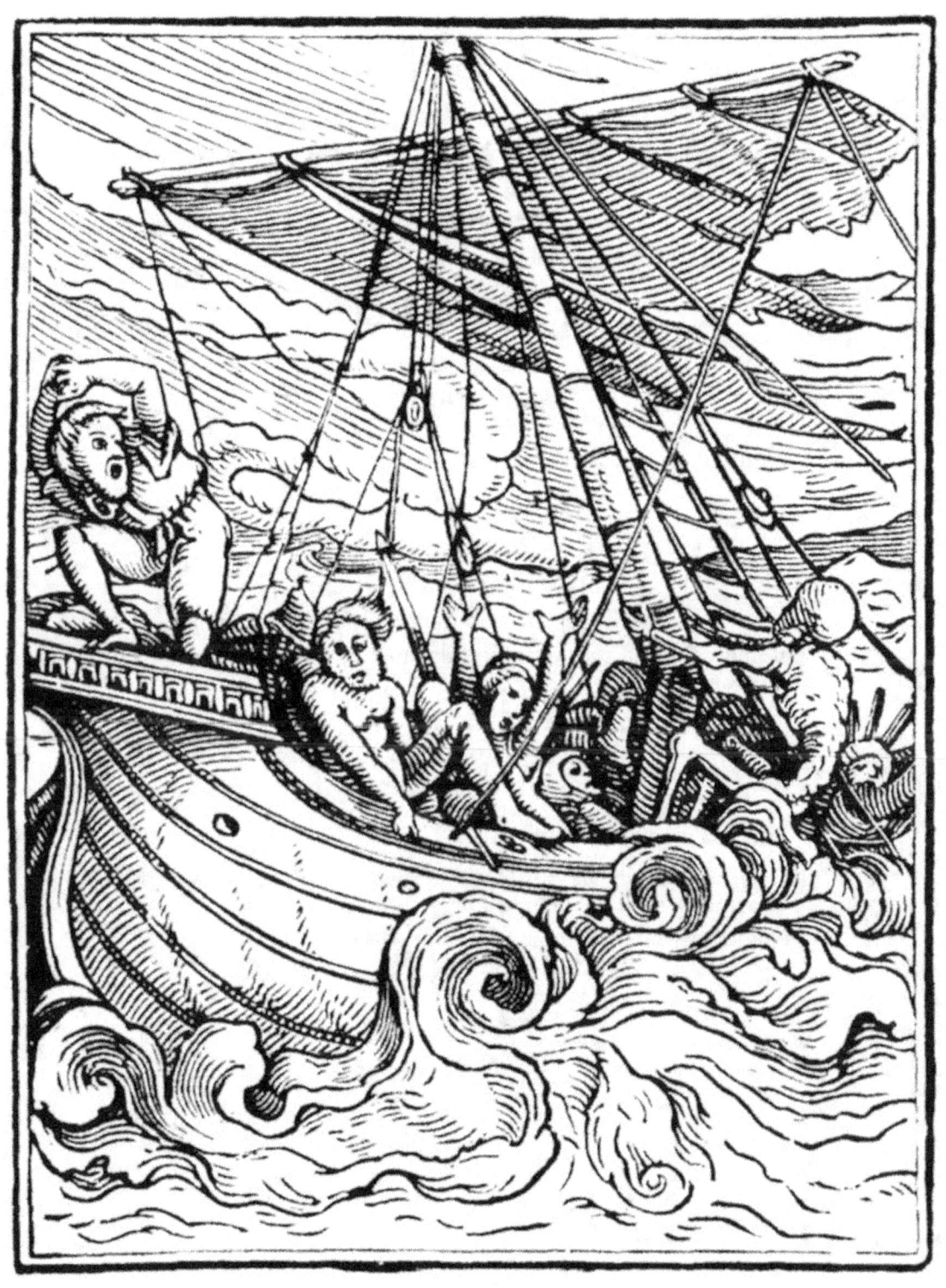

XXXI

THE KNIGHT

Der Ritter.

Death, in cuirass and chain-mail, runs him through the body.

In a moment shall they die, and the people shall be troubled
at midnight, and pass away; and the mighty shall be taken
away without hand.

Job 34:20

E'en in a moment shall they die,
At midnight shall men quake with fear,
The mighty shall not be pass'd by,
Nor know who thrusts the fatal spear.

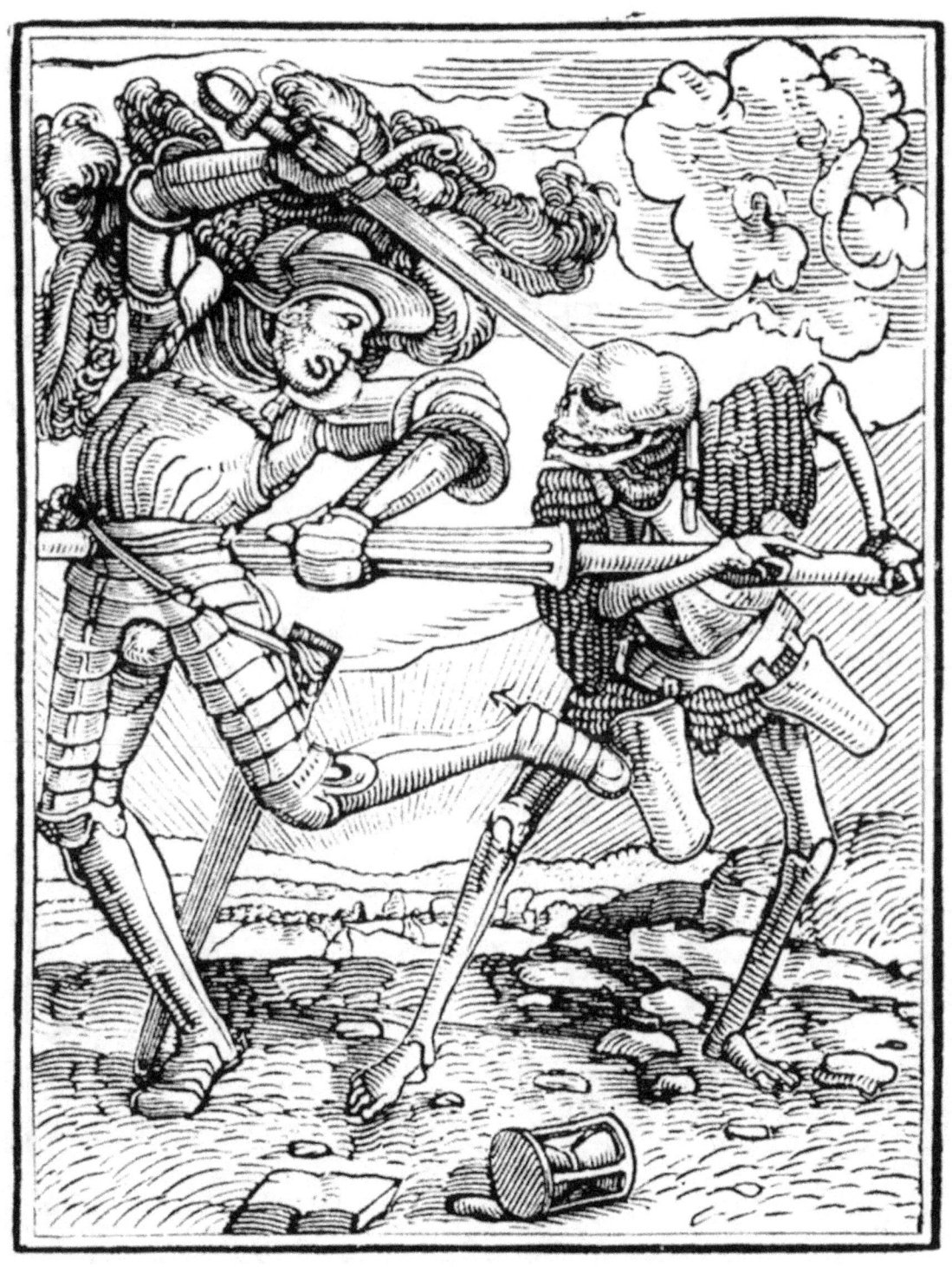

XXXII

THE COUNT

Der Graf.

Death, as a peasant with a flail, lifts away his back-piece.

For when he dieth he shall carry nothing away; his glory shall
not descend after him.

PSALM 49:17

Baubles and earthly pomps for ever flown,
Poor as the poorest he hath swiftly grown,
Yet shall good deeds, if any he hath done,
Remain his glory after he is gone.

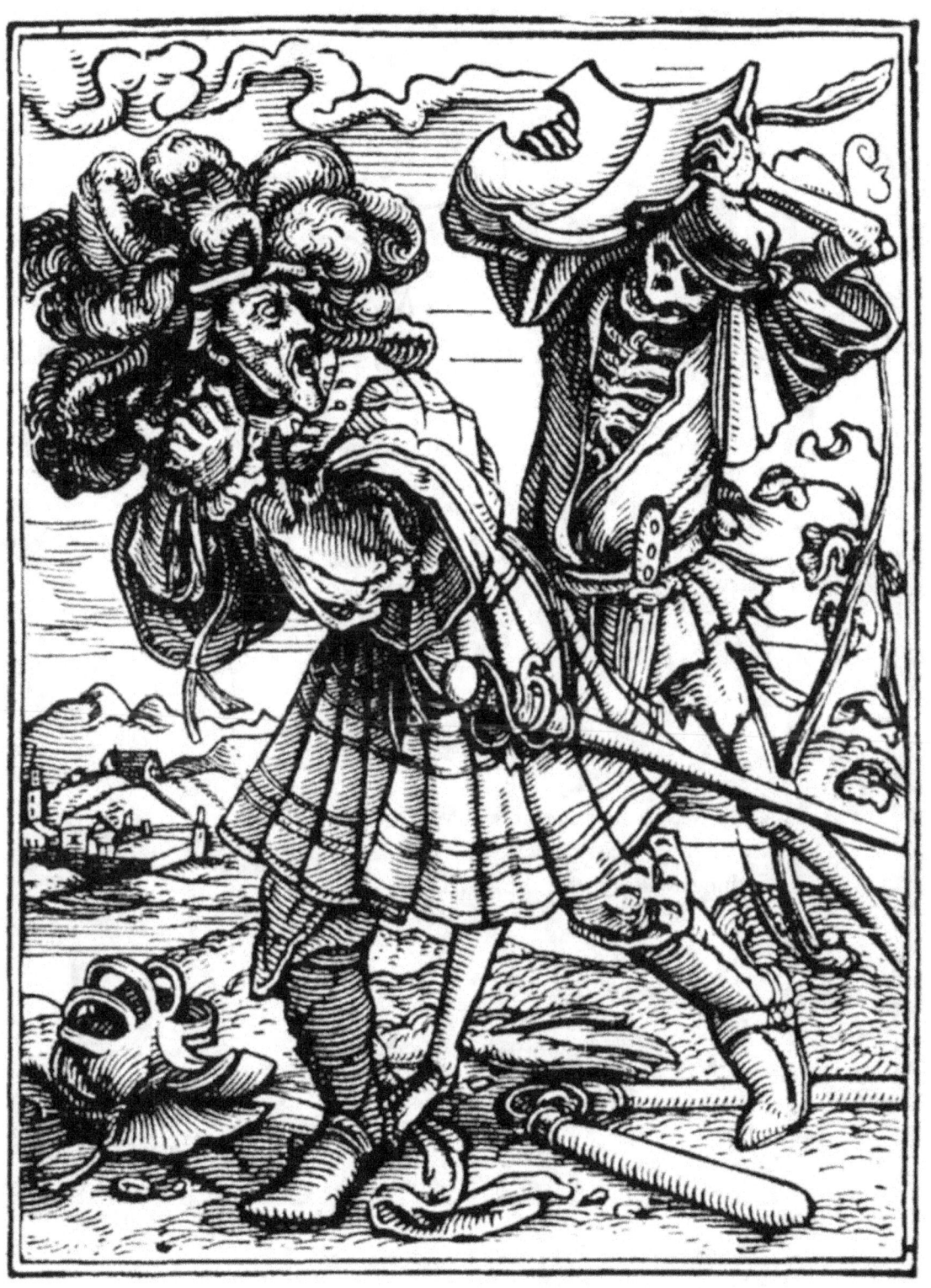

XXXIII

THE OLD MAN

Der Altmann.

Death, playing on a dulcimer, leads him into his grave.

My breath is corrupt, my days are extinct, the graves are ready
for me.

JOB 17:1

My spirit weakens day by day,
My life has reached the latest stave.
My latter days pass fast away—
Nothing awaits me but the grave.

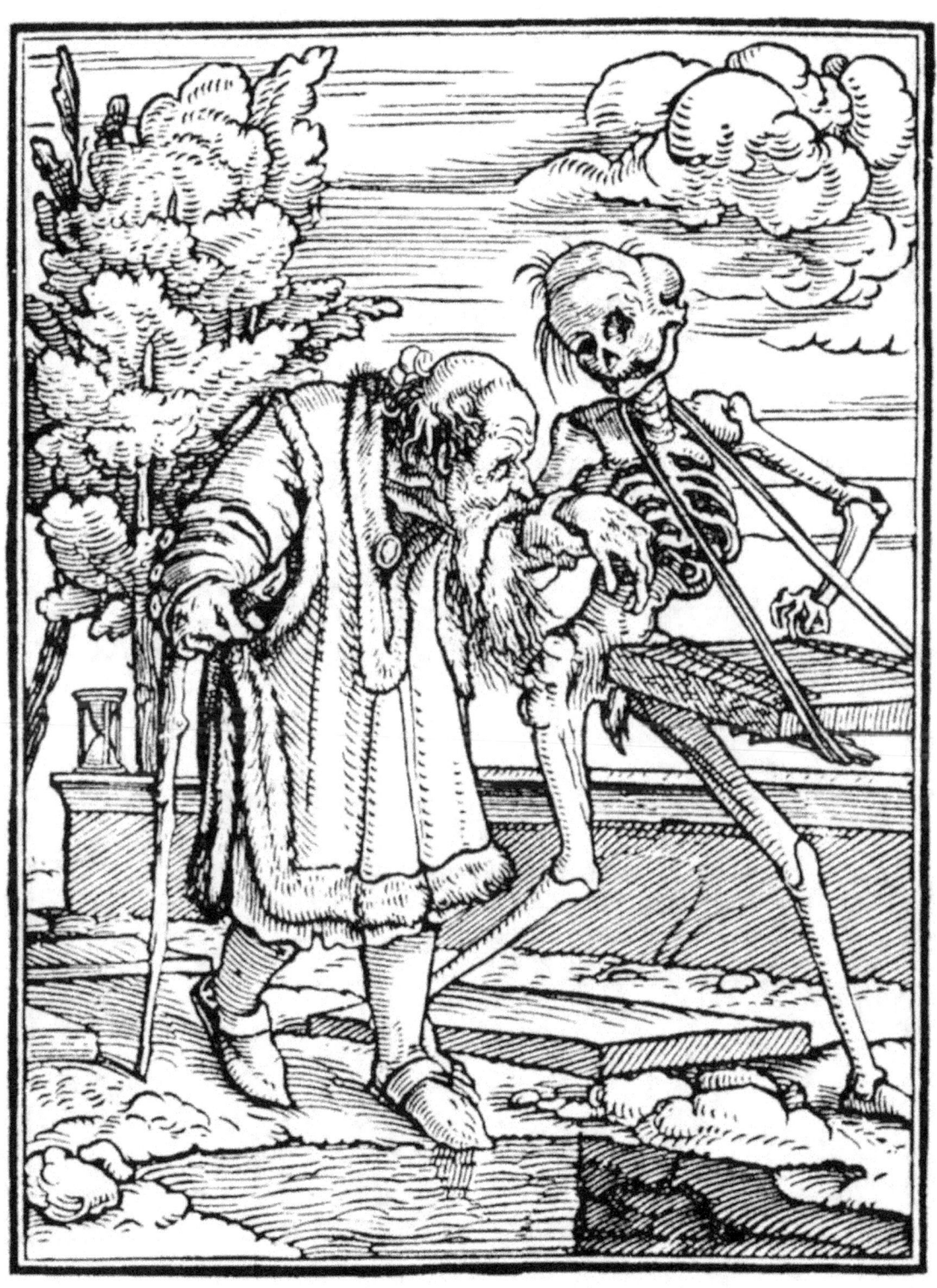

XXXIV

THE COUNTESS

Die Grafinn.

Death helps her at her tiring by decorating her with a necklet of dead men's bones.

They spend their days in wealth, and in a moment go down to the grave.

JOB 21:13

Their days on worldliness depend,
And pleasure, sought voluptuously:
Suddenly they to Hell descend,
Where joy is turned to misery.

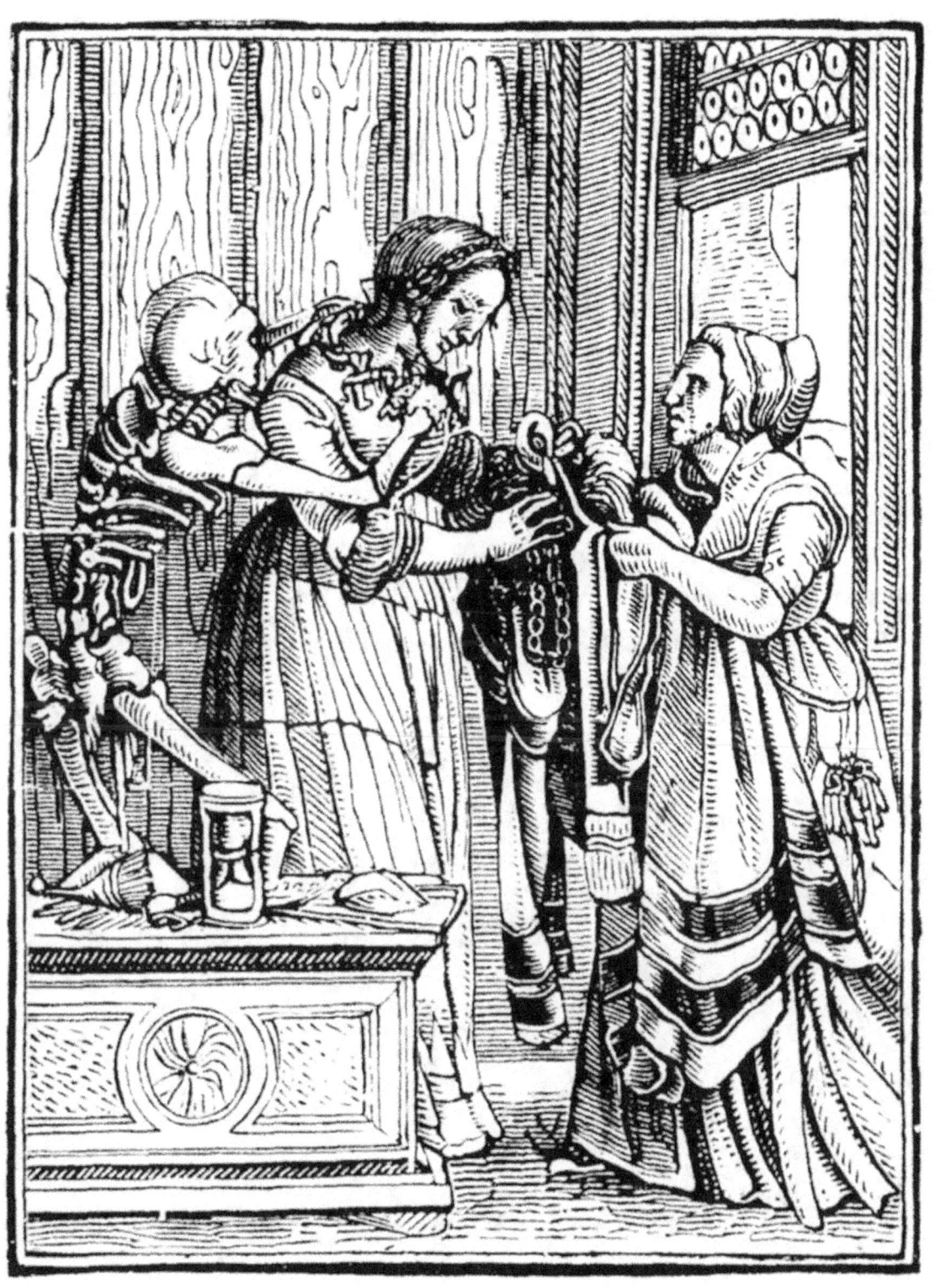

XXXV

THE NOBLE LADY, OR BRIDE

Die Edelfrau.

"Me et te sola mors separabit"—says the motto. And Death already dances before her.

The Lord do so to me, and more also, if aught but death part thee and me.

RUTH 1:17

The love by which they are united,
By faith should teach them, ere too late,
That soon such unions may be blighted,
And Death step in to separate.

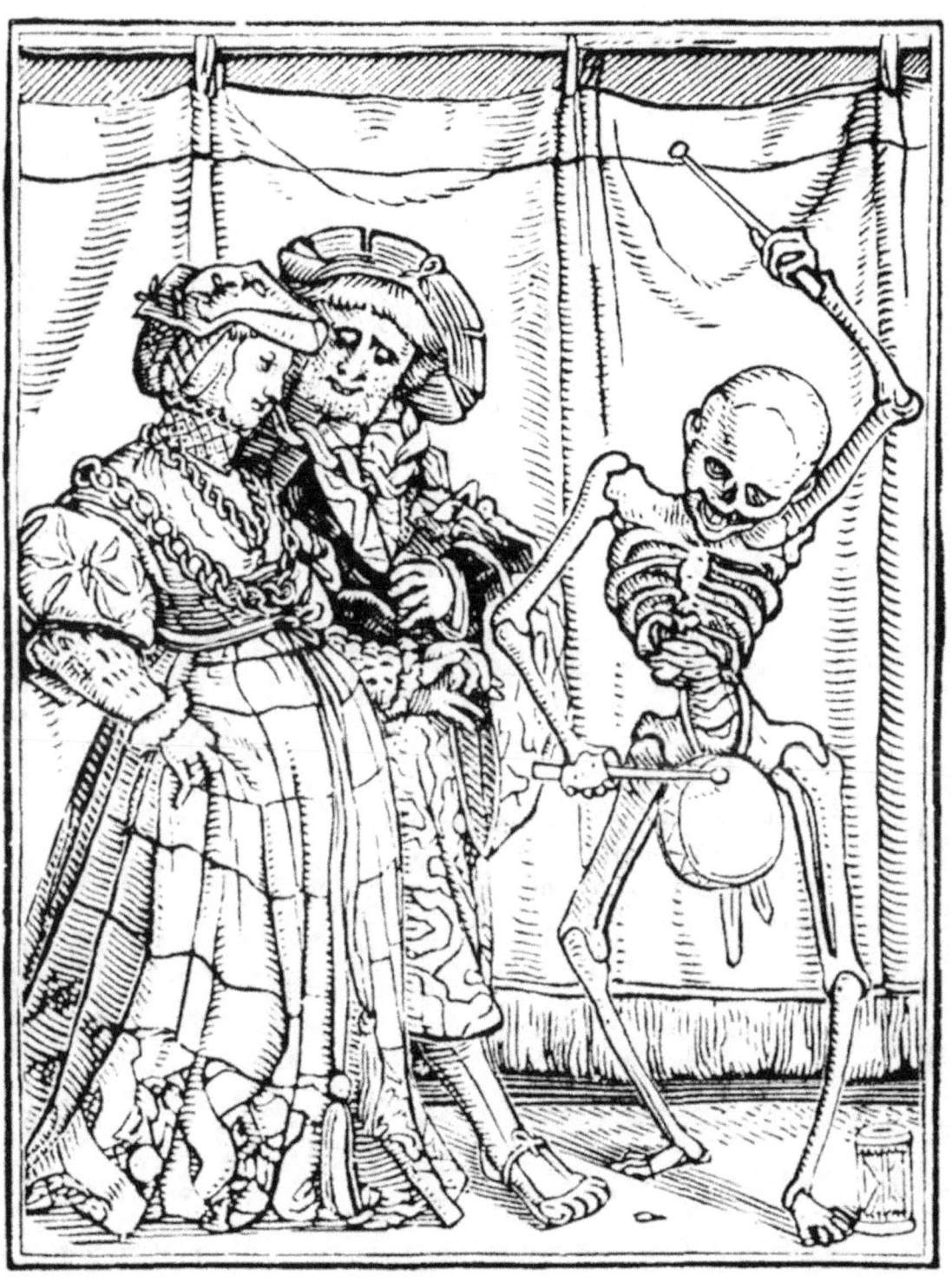

XXXVI

THE DUCHESS

Die Herzoginn.

Death seizes her in bed, while his fellow plays the fiddle.

Thou shalt not come down from that bed on which thou are
gone up, but shall surely die.

2 Kings 1:4

Thou ne'er shalt leave that bed of down,
On which thou art about to lie.
Death round thee hath his meshes thrown,
And, vain one! Thou must surely die.

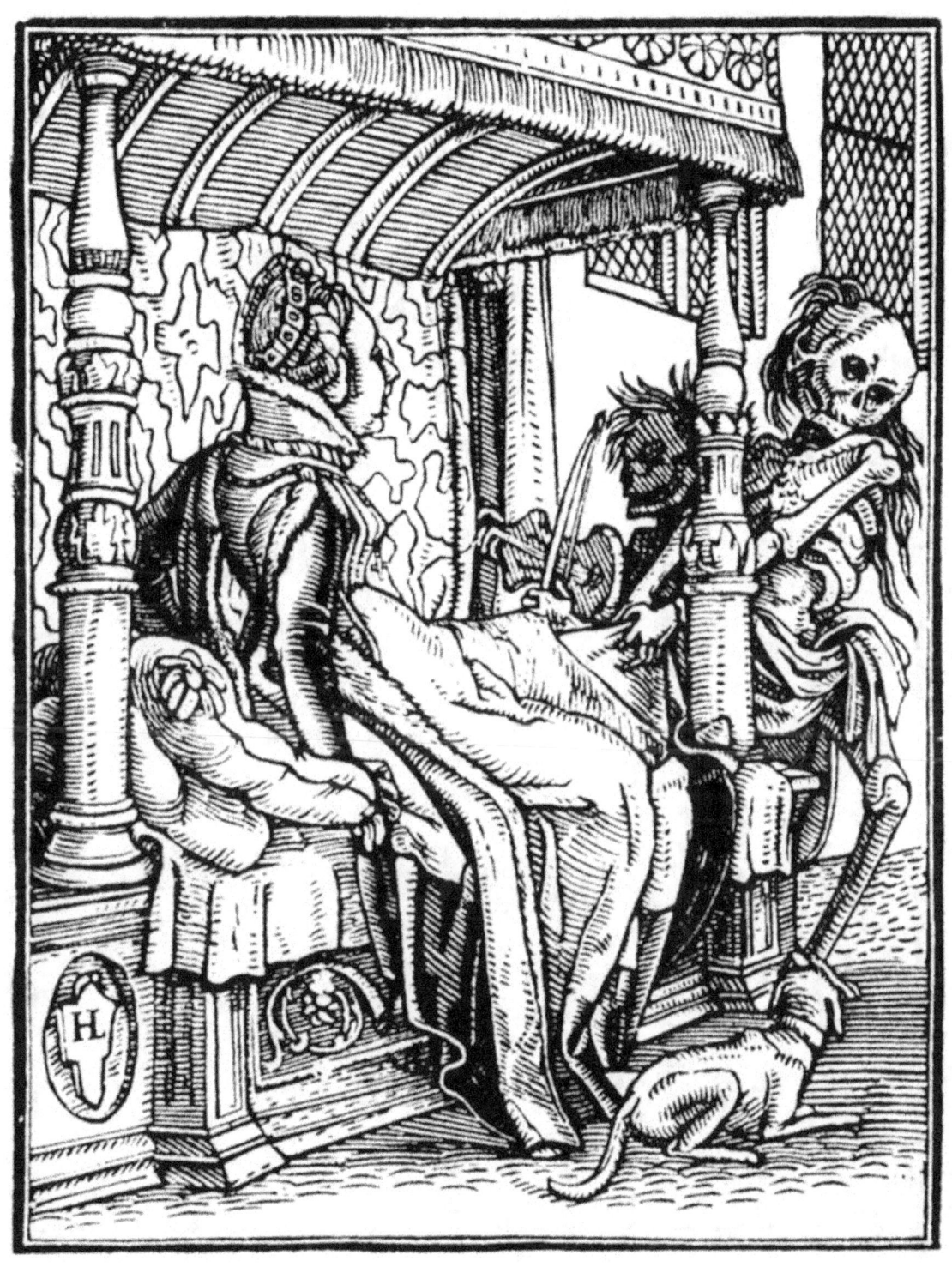

XXXVII

THE PEDLAR

Der Kramer.

Death stops him on the road with his wares at his back.

Come unto me, all ye that labour and are heavy laden, and I
will give you rest.

MATTHEW 11:28

Cease from thy tramping—follow me;
Thou'rt heavy laden for the road.
Ay! Let the fair and market be;
I will thy weighty pack unload.

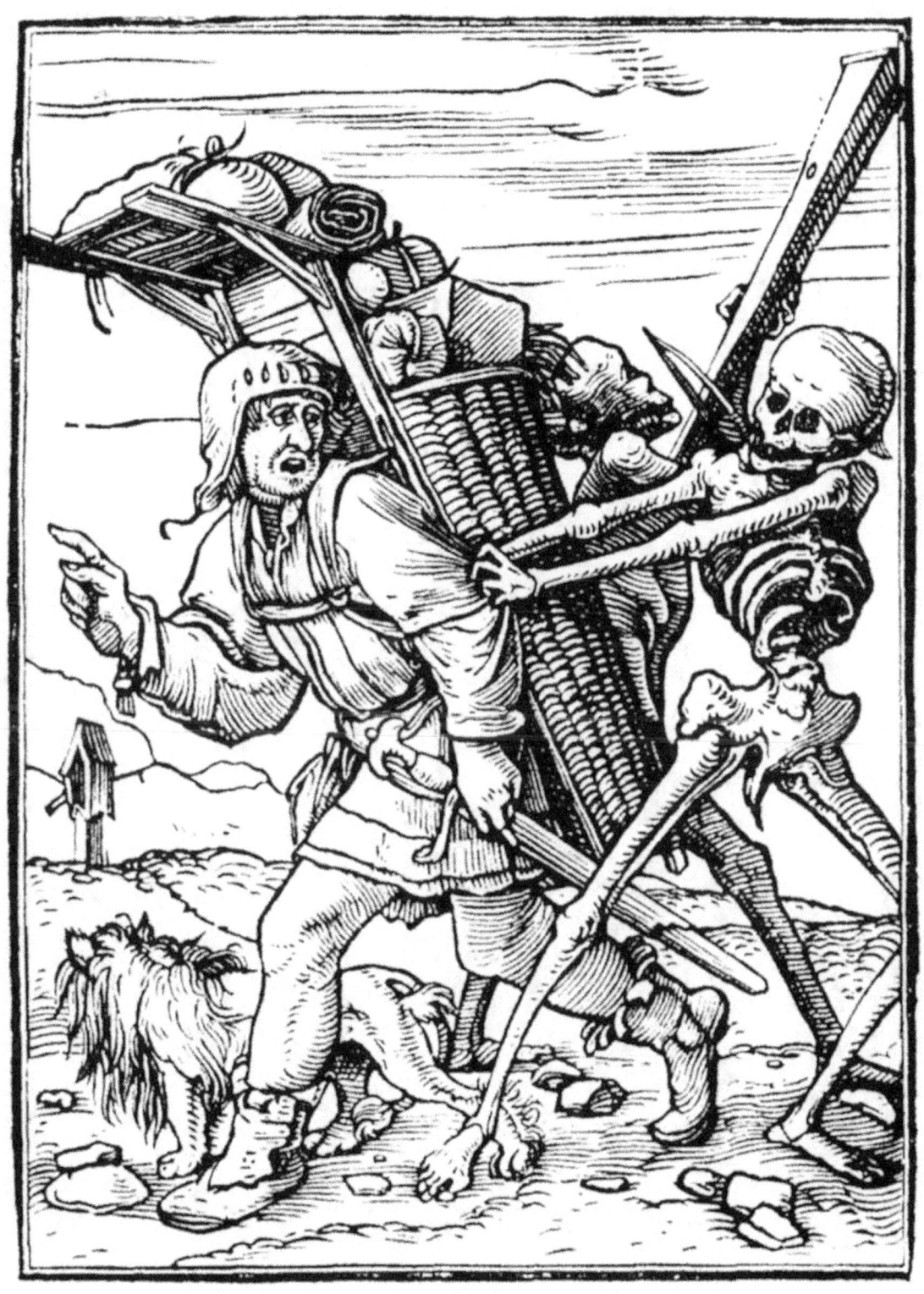

XXXVIII

THE PLOUGHMAN

Der Ackermann.

Death runs at the horses' sides as the sun sinks, and the furrows are completed.

In the sweat of thy face shalt thou eat bread, till thou return
unto the ground.

GENESIS 3:19

With sweating brown and horny hand,
Thou work'st ere thou mayst break thy fast:
Enough thou'st till'd and delved the land;
Death comes to speed thy plough at last.

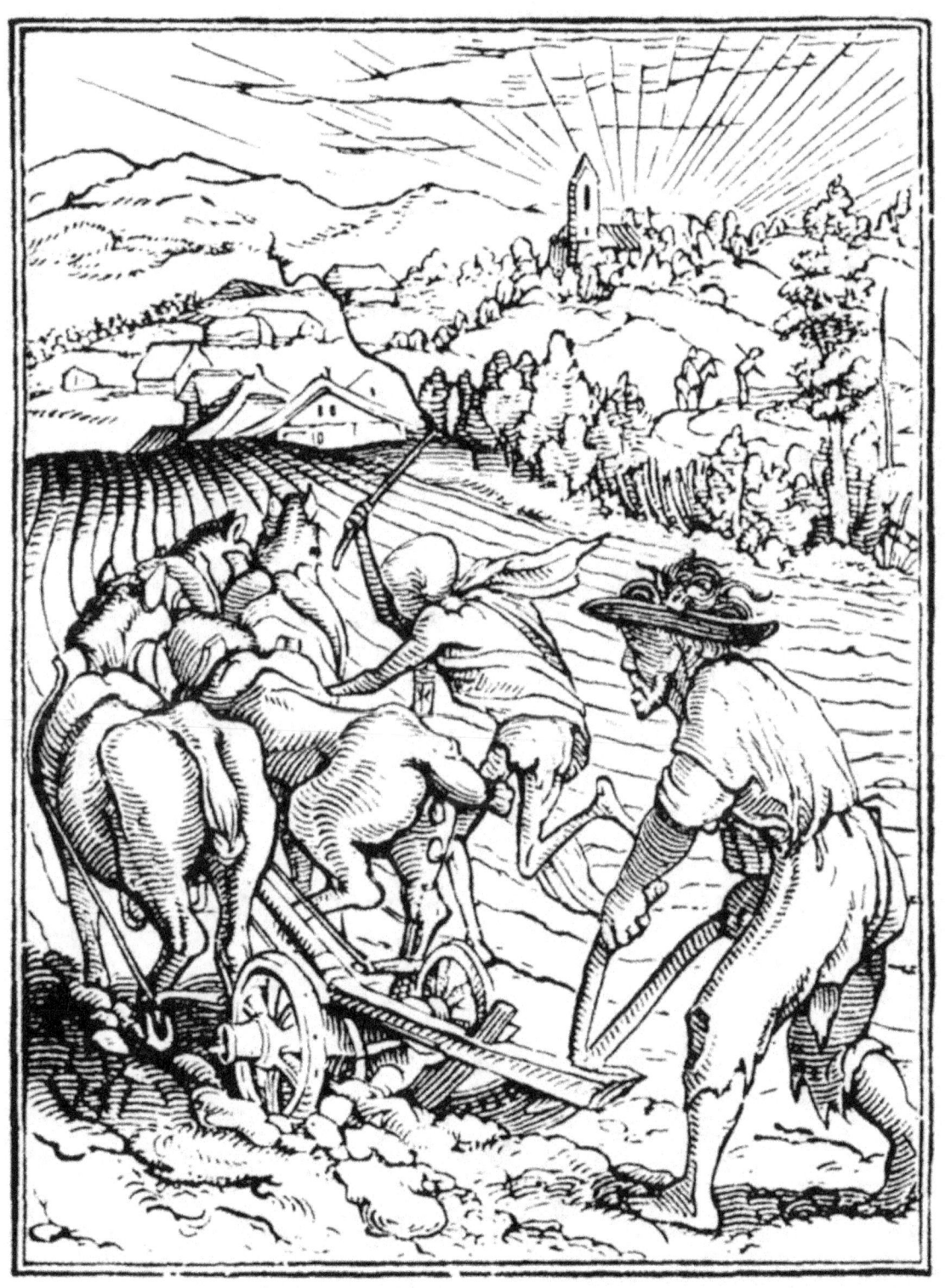

XXXIX

❧

THE YOUNG CHILD

Das Junge Kind.

As the meagre cottage meal is preparing, Death steals the youngest child.

Man that is born of a woman is of few days, and full of
trouble. He cometh forth like a flower, and is cut down; he
fleeth also as a shadow, and continuith not.

JOB 14:1 & 2

Man that is born of woman has
Few days, made difficult with woes:
He passes, even as flowers pass;
He comes, and like a shadow goes.

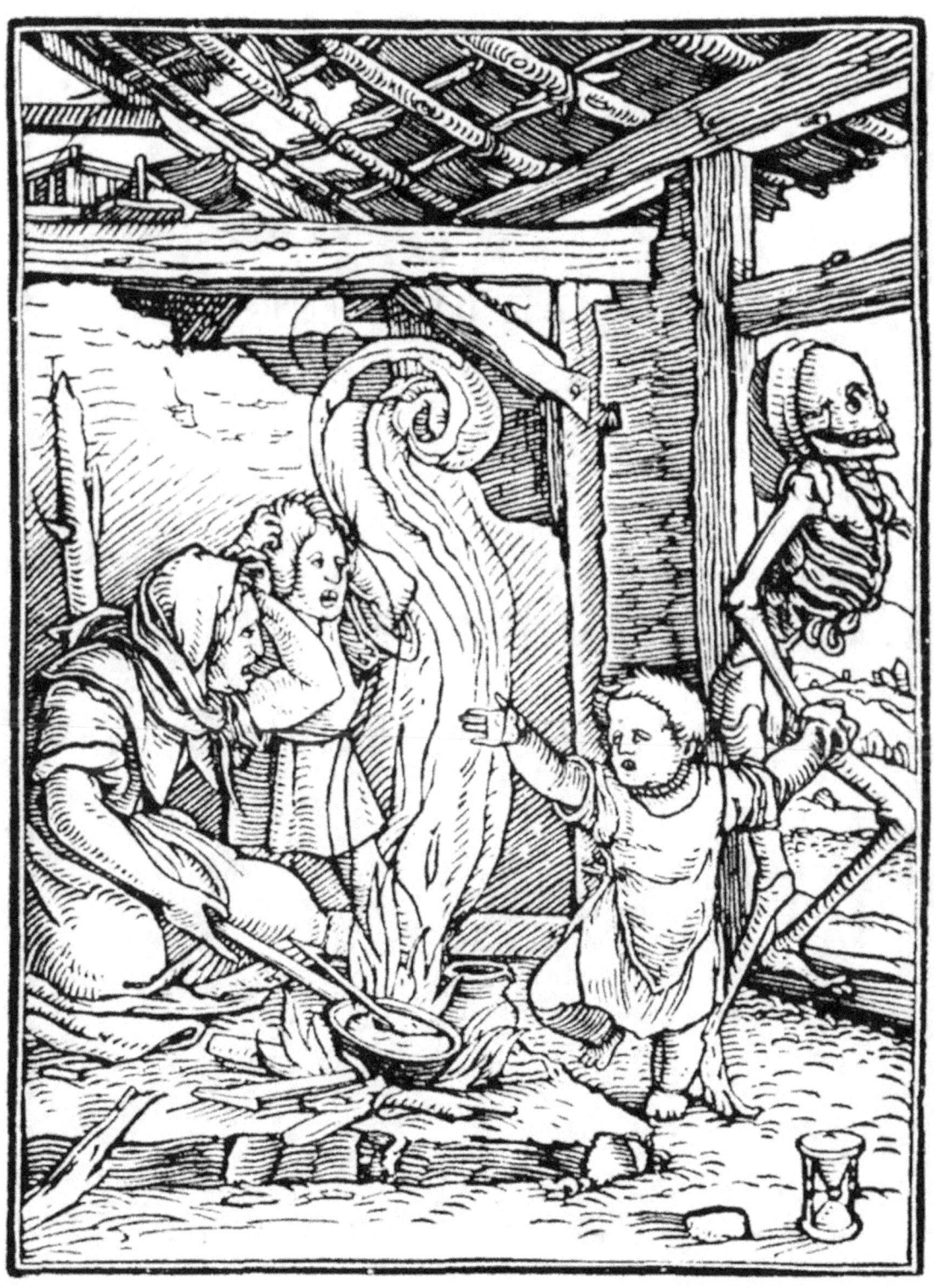

XL

·—•—·

THE LAST JUDGMENT

Das jüngste Gericht.

"Omnes stabimus ante tribunal Domini."

·—•—·

So then every one of us shall give account of himself to God.

ROMANS 14:12

Watch therefore: for ye know not what hour your Lord doth come.

MATTHEW 24:42

Before the mighty Judge's chair
Comes reckoning for each man alive;
Fear, then, the judgments rendered there:
You know not when He will arrive.

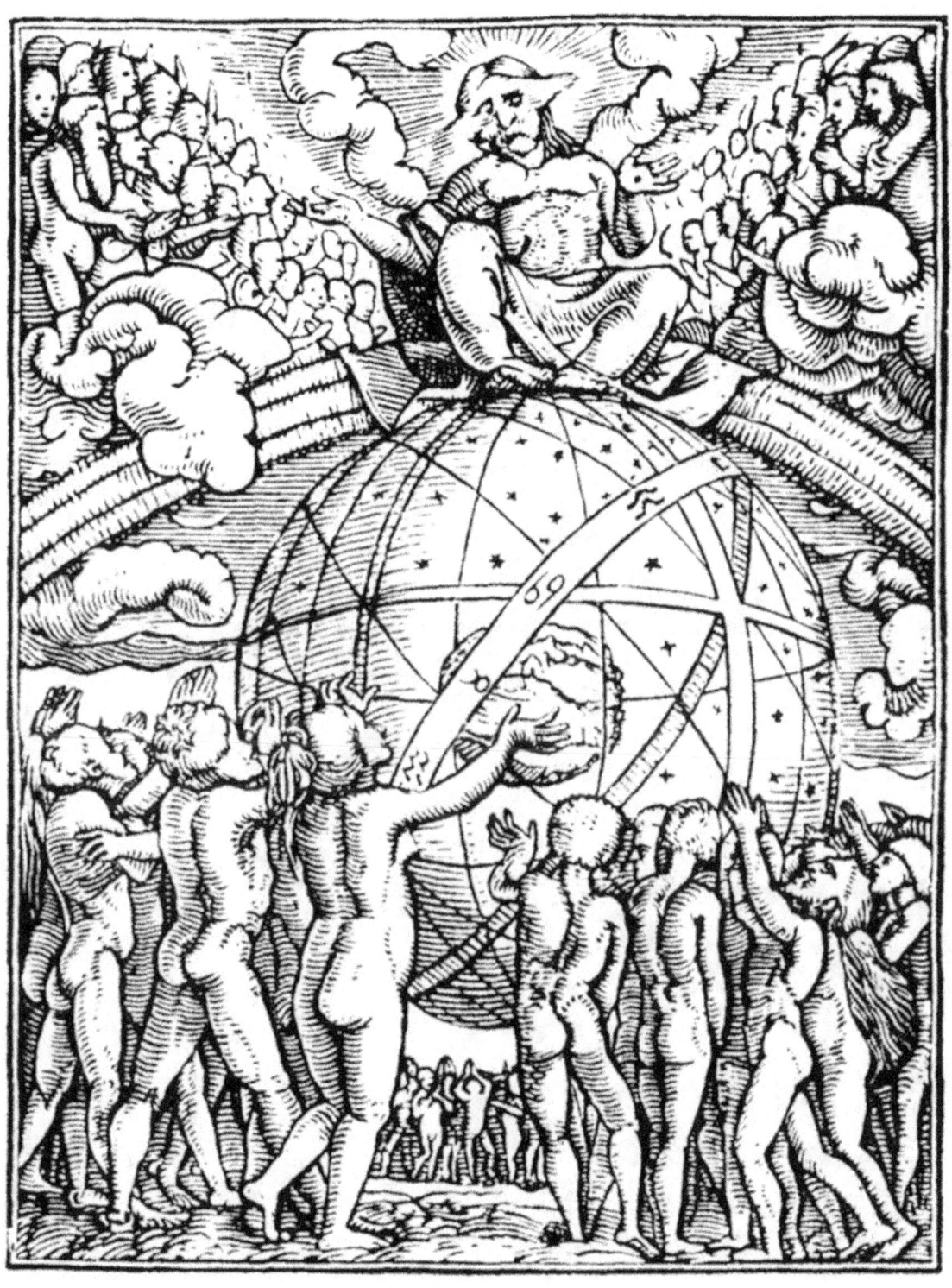

XLI

THE ESCUTCHEON OF DEATH

Die Wappen des Todes.

The supporters represent Holbein and his wife.

Remember the end, and thou shalt neve do amiss.

ECCLESIASTICUS 7:36

If you would lead a sinless life,
Then keep this scene in constant view,
And you will have no toil or strife
When long repose as come for you.

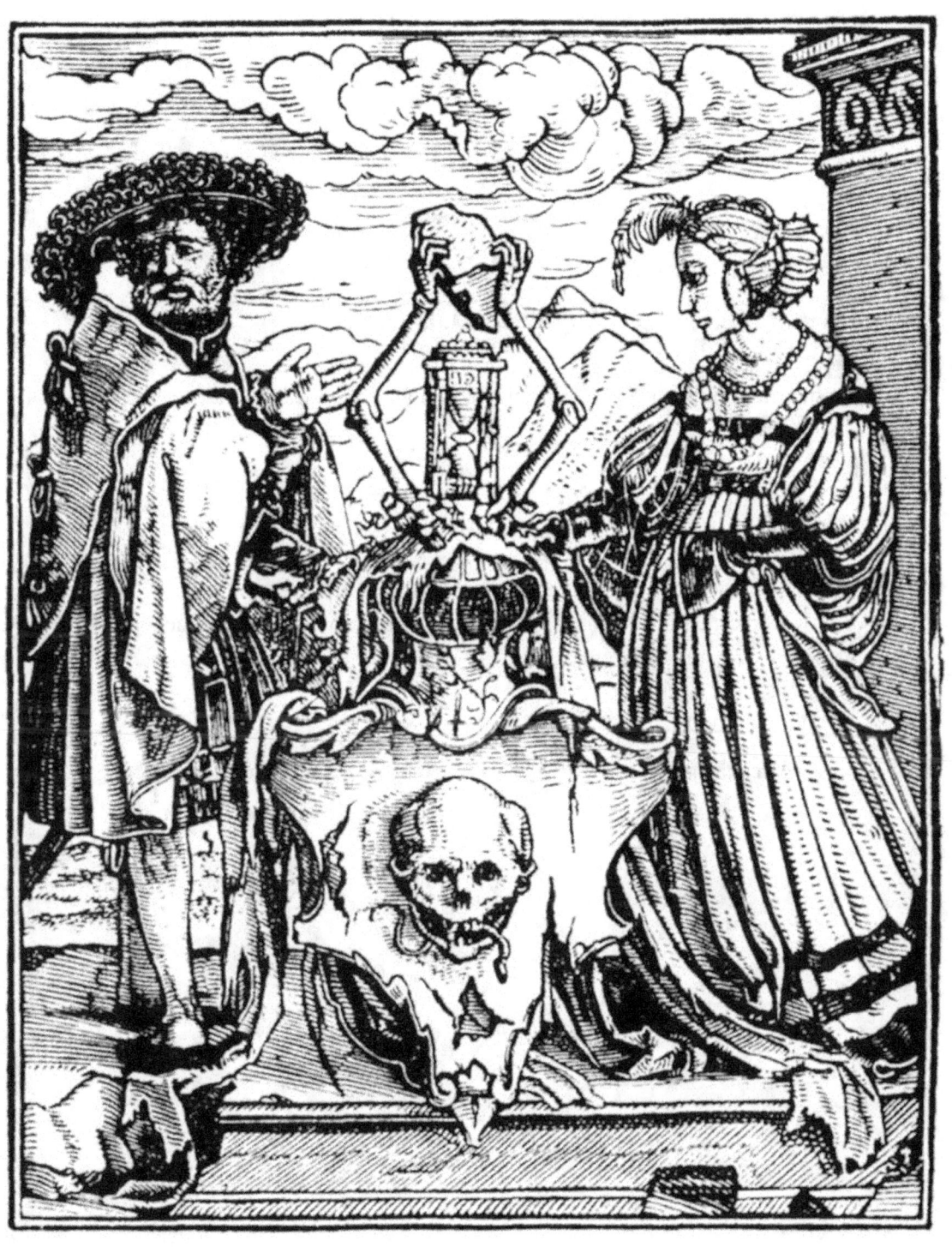

XLII

—◆—

THE SOLDIER

Death, armed only with a bone and shield, fights with the Soldier on the field of battle.

———◆———

But when a stronger than he shall come upon him, and overcome him, he taketh from him all his armour wherein he trusted, and divideth his spoils.

LUKE 11:23

After the game, the King and the pawn go into the same box.

—ITALIAN SAYING

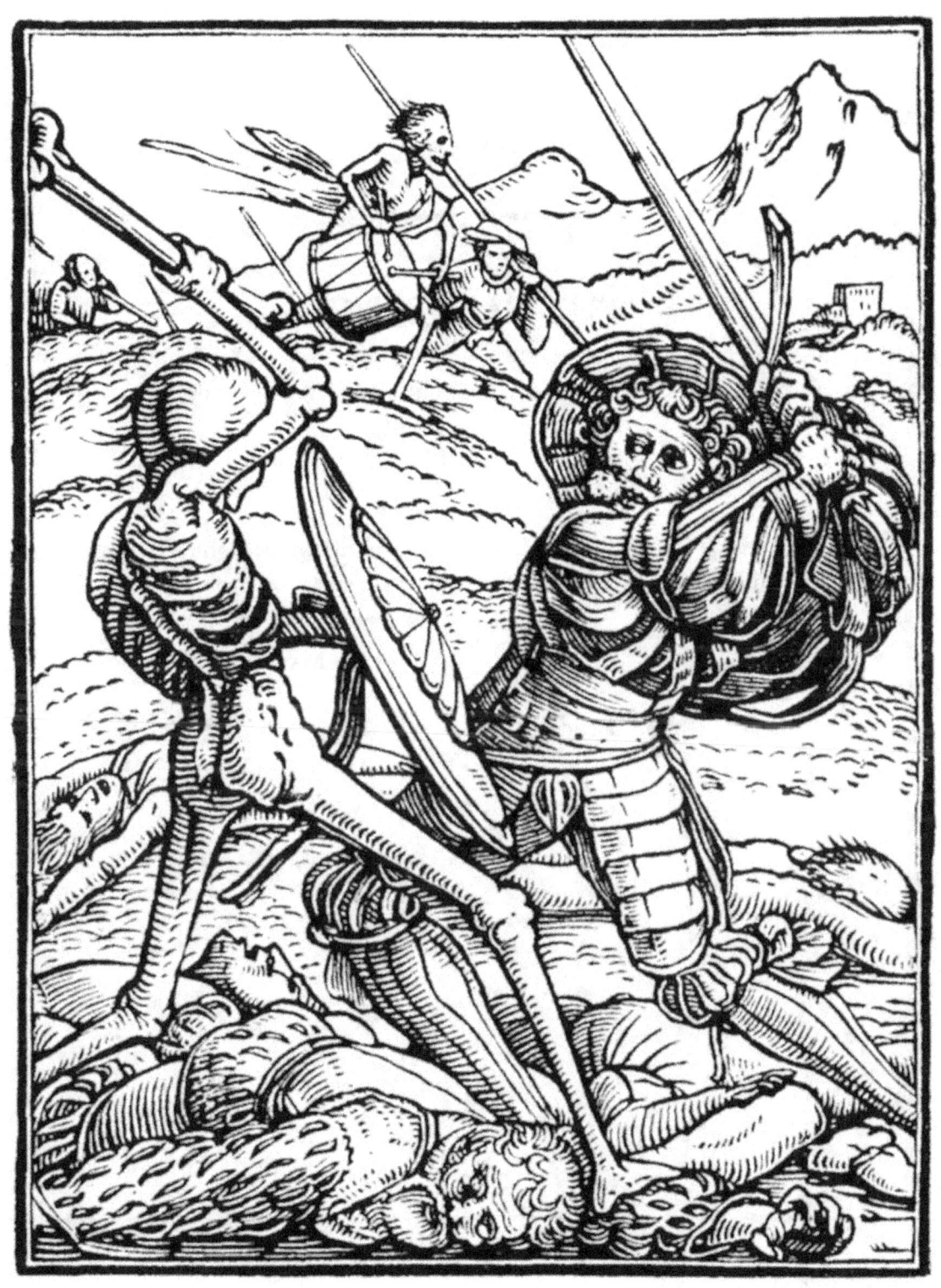

XLIII

THE GAMESTER

Death and the Devil seize upon the Gambler at his cards.

For what is a man profited, if he shall gain the whole world, and lose his own soul? or what shall a man give in exchange for his soul?

MATTHEW 16:26

Death keeps no calendar.

—ENGLISH SAYING

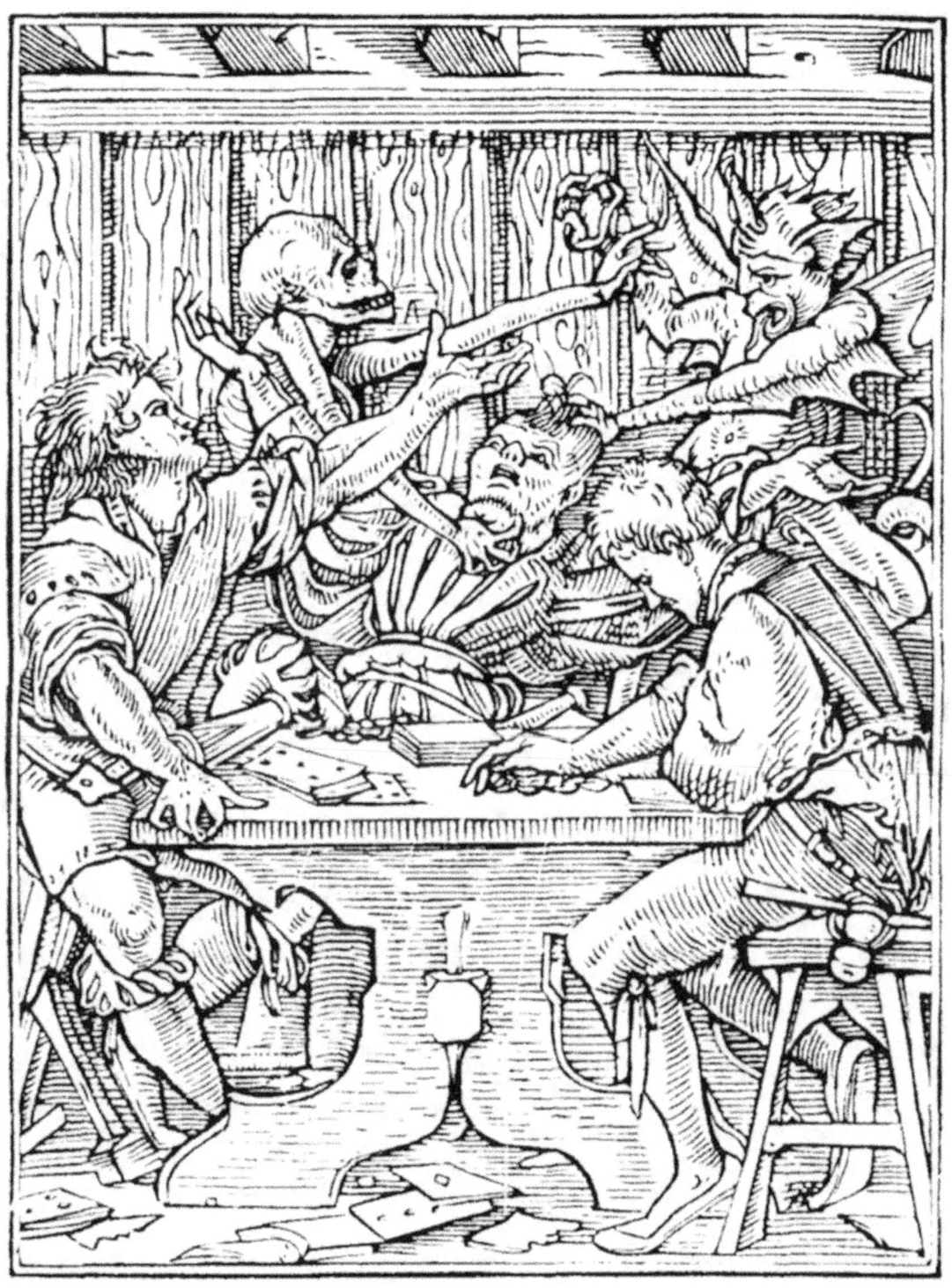

XLIV

—❦—

THE DRUNKARD

Men and women carouse: down the throat of one bloated fellow Death pours the wine.

———•———

And be not drunk with wine, wherein is excess; but be filled with the Spirit.

EPHESIANS 5:18

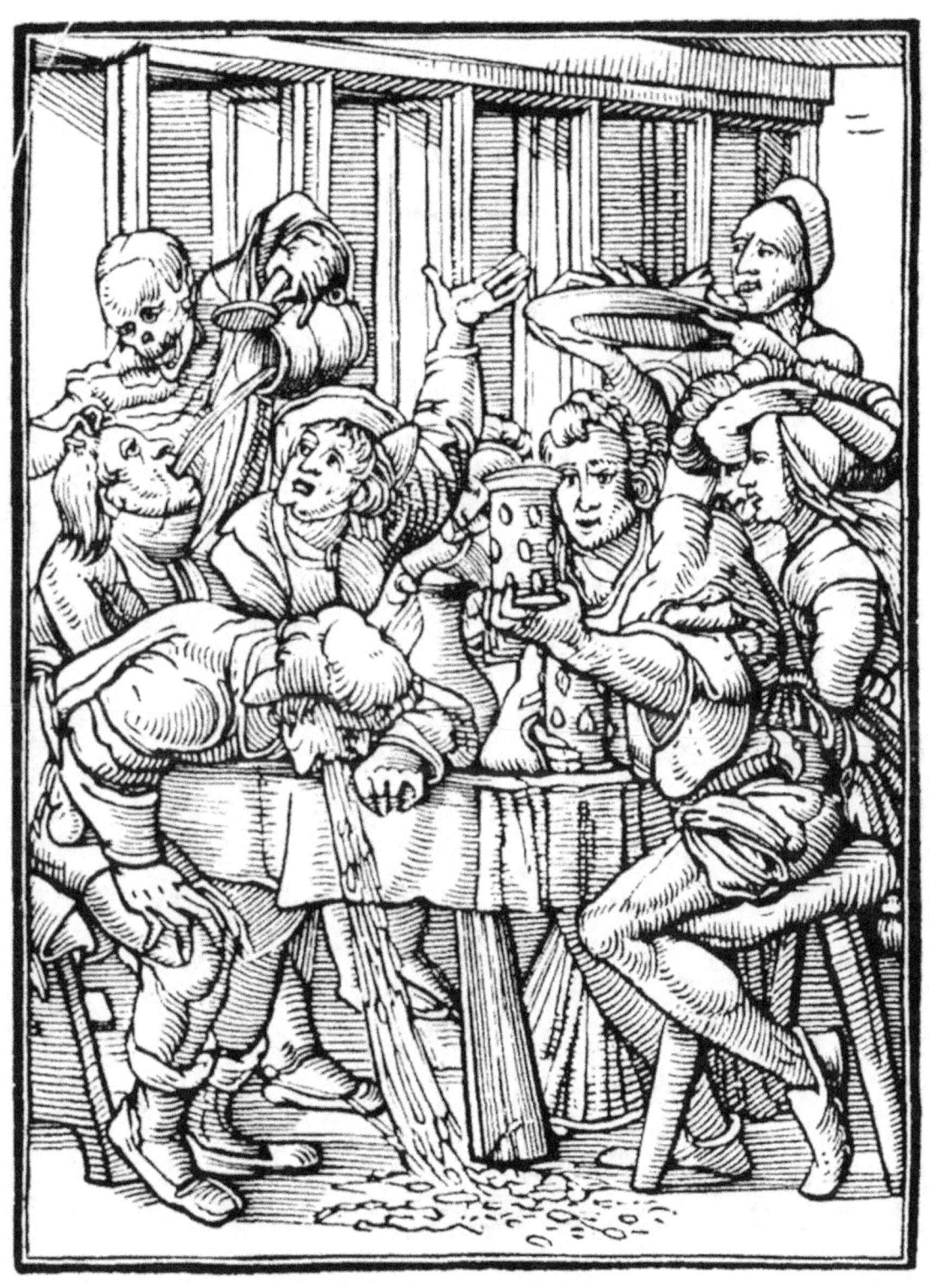

XLV

THE FOOL

The Fool dances along the highway with Death, who plays the bagpipes.

He followed her immediately, as an ox goes to the slaughter,
as a fool stepping into a noose.

PROVERB 7:22

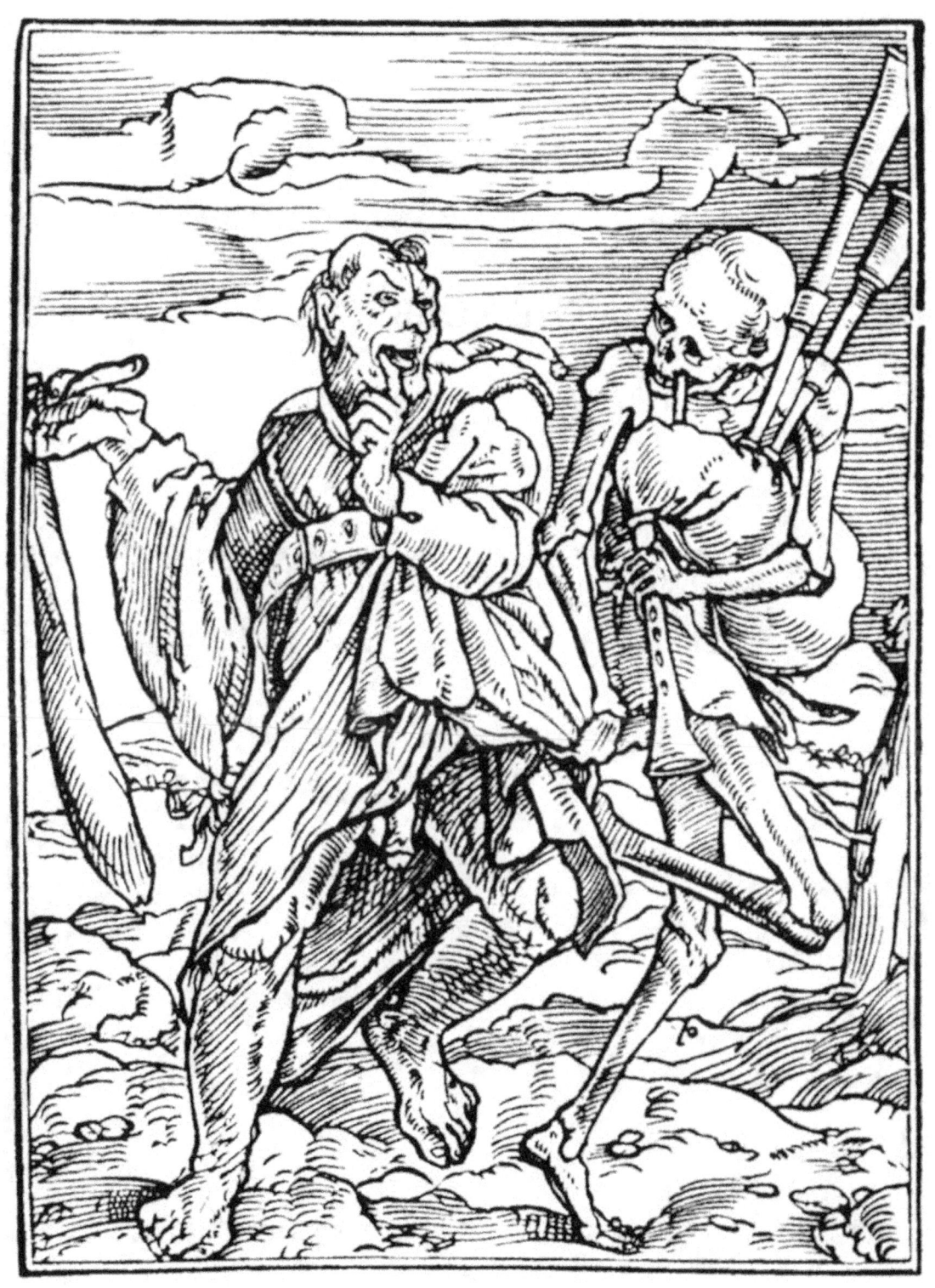

XLVI

THE ROBBER

Death seizes the Robber in the act of pillage.

For the grave cannot praise thee, death can not celebrate thee:
they that go down into the pit cannot hope for thy truth.

ISAIAH 38:18

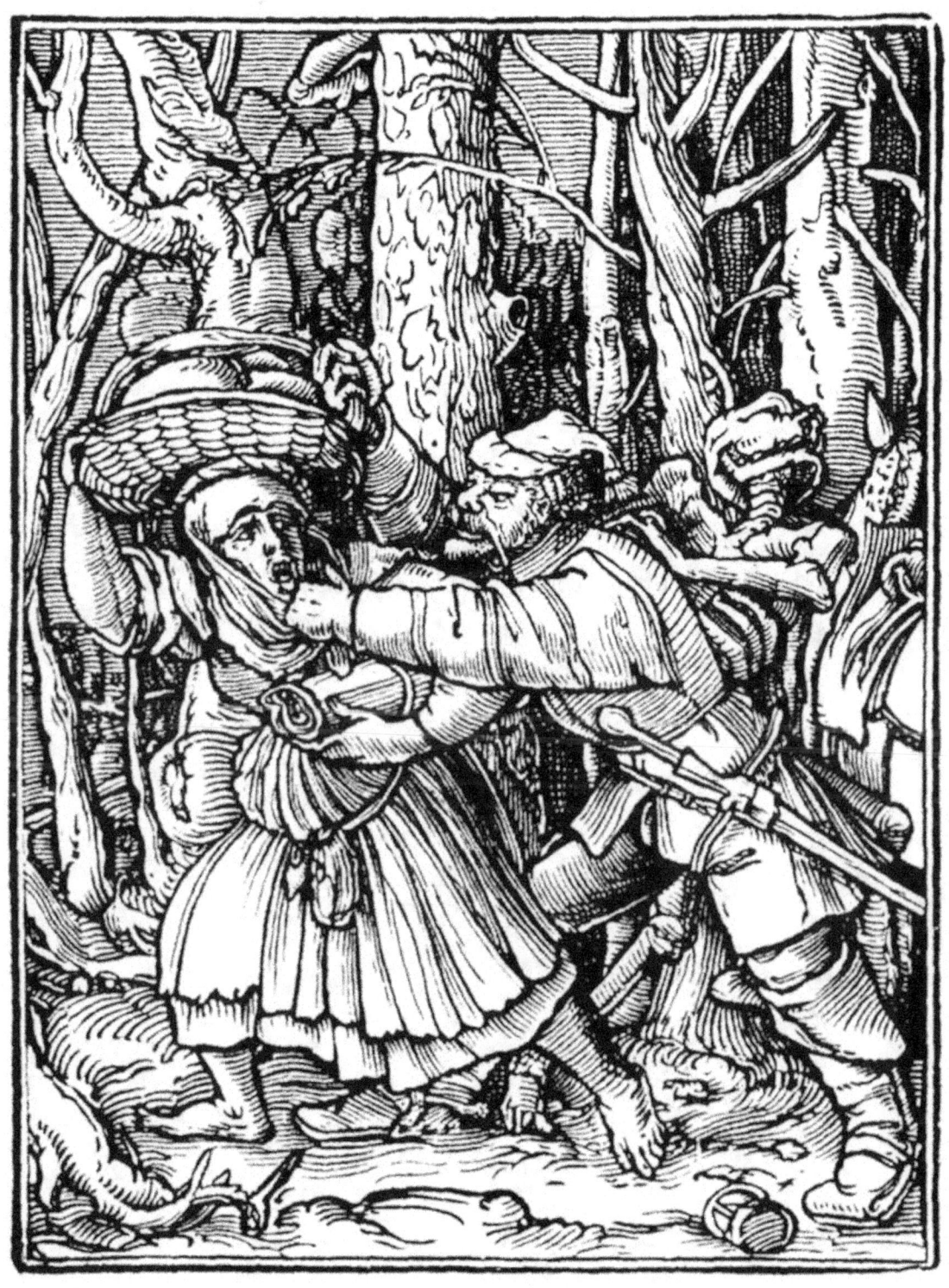

XLVII

THE BLIND MAN

Death leads the Blind Man by his staff.

Let them alone: they be blind leaders of the blind. And if the blind lead the blind, both shall fall into the ditch.

MATTHEW 15:14

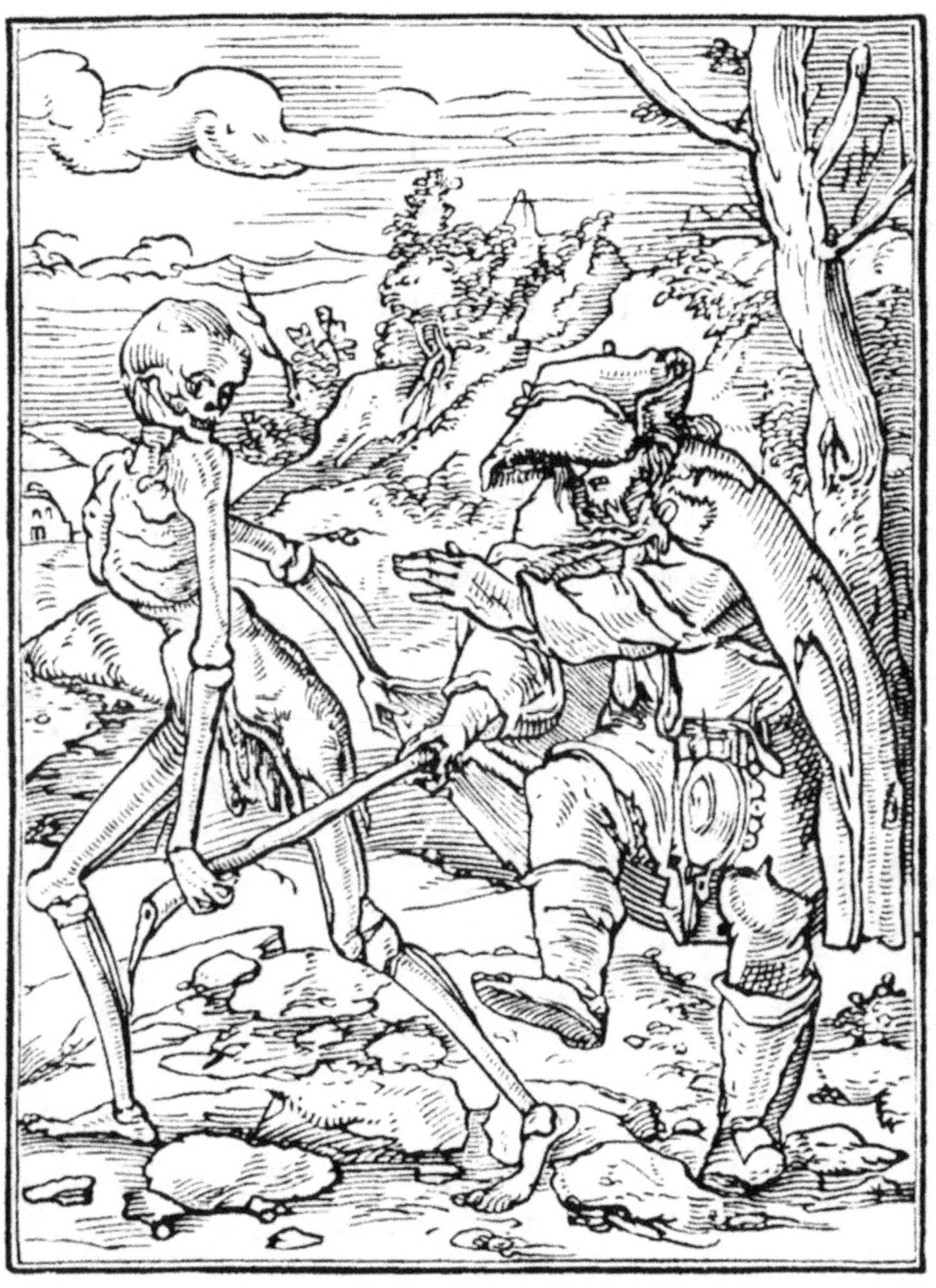

XLVIII

***

THE WAGGONER

The waggon is overturned; one Death carries off a wheel, the other loosens the fastening of a cask.

***

… and he sunk down in his chariot.

2 KINGS 9:24

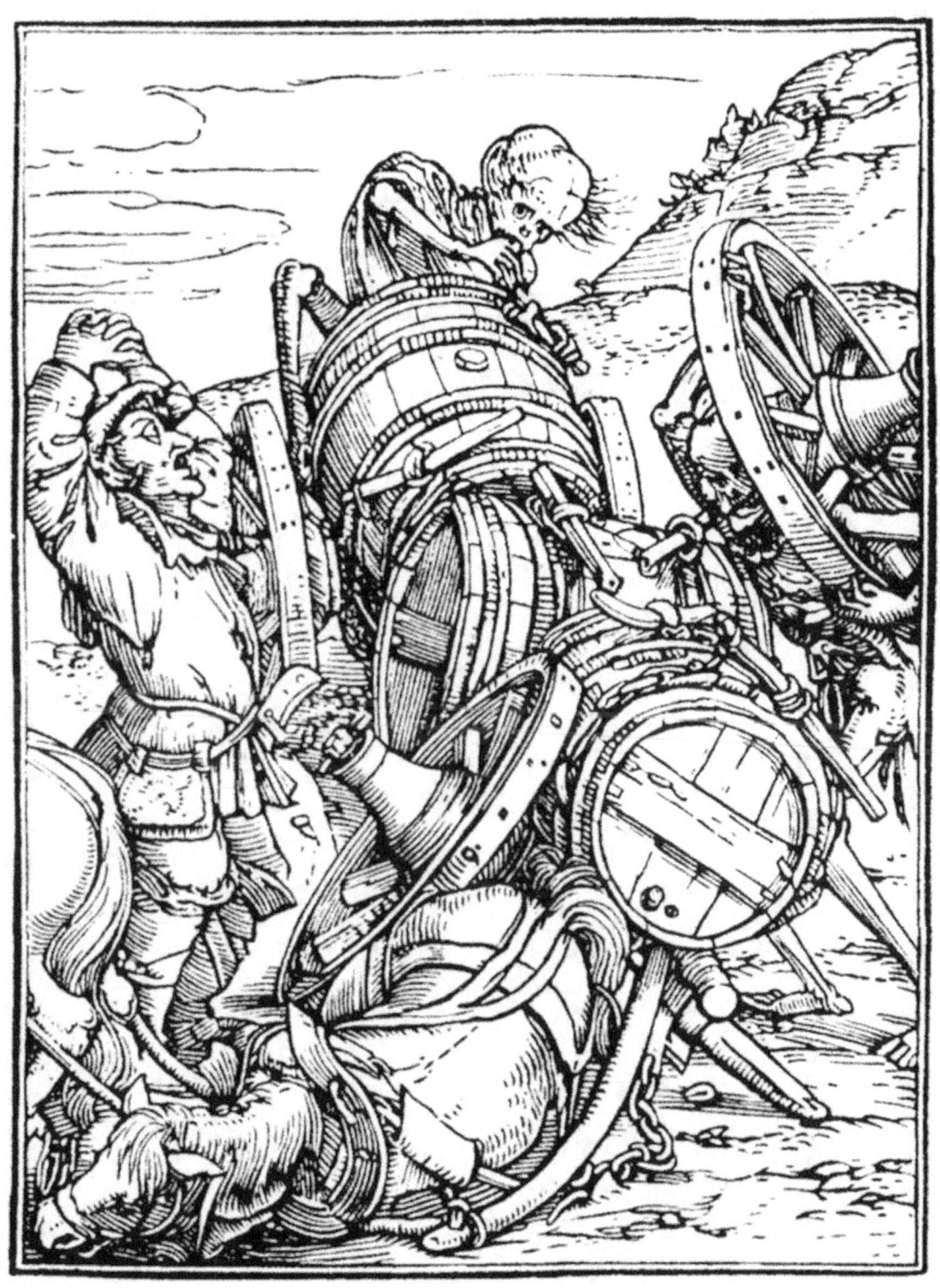

XLIX

THE BEGGAR

The Beggar, lying on straw outside the city, cries in vain for Death.

O wretched man that I am! who shall deliver me from the body of this death?

ROMANS 7:24

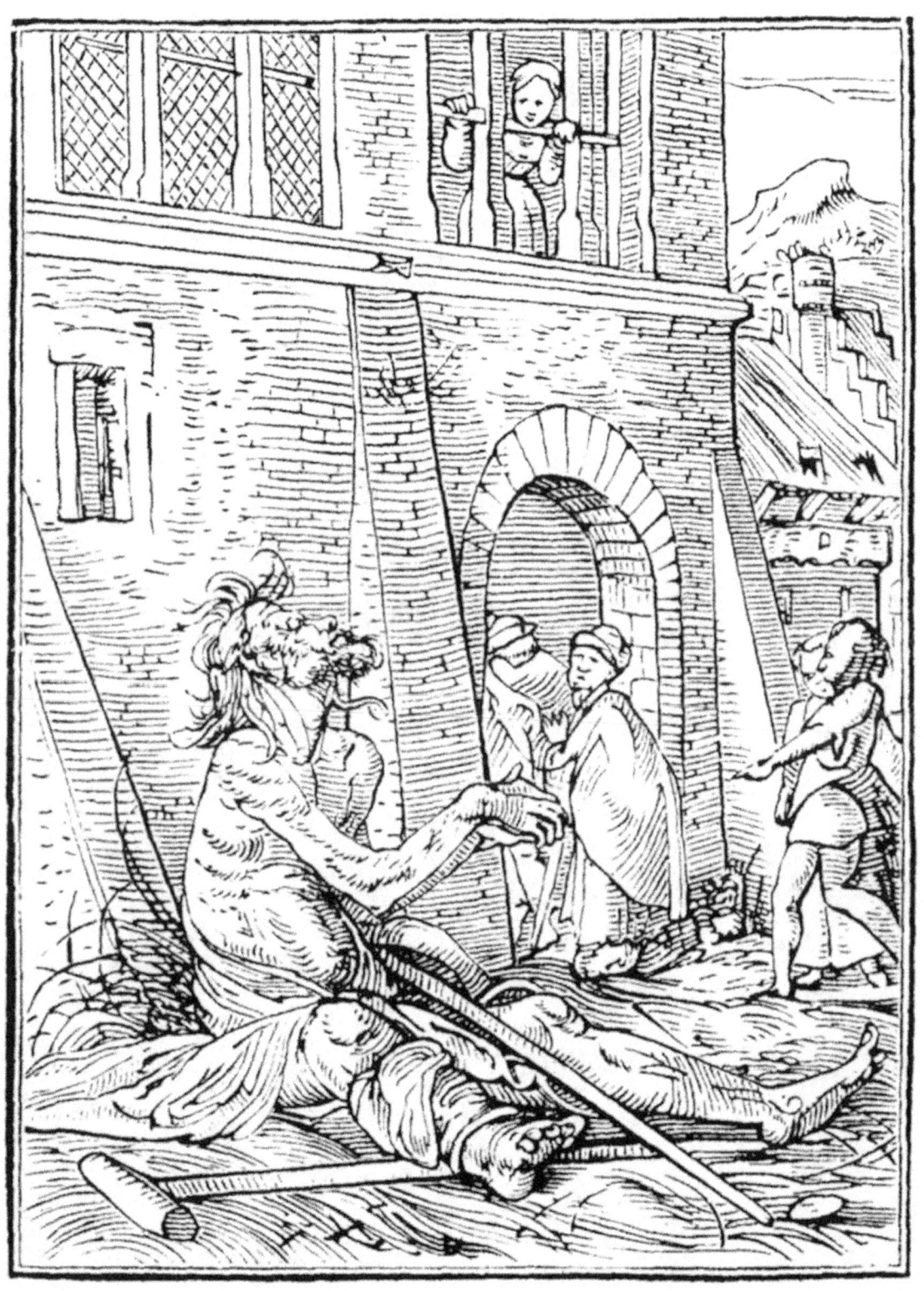

www.ingramcontent.com/pod-product-compliance
Lightning Source LLC
Chambersburg PA
CBHW081301170526
45165CB00011B/3371